FIGHT SCENES

FIGHT SCENES

Greg Bottoms

Illustrated by David Powell

Counterpoint
Berkeley

Author's Note: This book has its origin in the recall of actual people, things, and events from my actual life during an actual year in an actual place. My interest is in reality. But memory is fluid, the past is not recoverable as a whole, and any artistic representation of a time twenty-five years gone, regardless of intention, is probably best read as a work of fiction. Names and distinguishing characteristics have been altered.

Portions of this book, in different form, first appeared in *Arts & Letters, Brevity, North American Review,* and *River Teeth.*

Library of Congress Cataloging-in-Publication Data

Bottoms, Greg
  Fight scenes / Greg Bottoms ; illustrated by David Powell
  p. cm.
  1. Problem families—Fiction. I. Title.
   PS3602.O88F54 2008
   813'.6—dc22
                    2008012041

ISBN (10) 1-59376-129-5
ISBN (13) 978-1-59376-129-5

Cover design and interior illustrations by David Powell
Interior design by Neuwirth & Associates
Printed in the United States of America

Counterpoint
2117 Fourth Street
Suite D
Berkeley, CA 94710

www.counterpointpress.com

Distributed by Publishers Group West

10 9 8 7 6 5 4 3 2 1

I'm going to ramble on a little tonight about my own past, not as though it were my own past exactly, but as a subject for fiction ... For it is important to ask, I think, where did these people I'm talking about come from and where did they get their peculiar school of ethics? What was its origin? What did it mean to them? What did it come out of? What function did it serve and why was it happening here? And why were they living where they were and what was it doing to them? All these things which sociologists think they can find out and haven't managed to do, which no chart can tell us.

—James Baldwin,
"Notes for a Hypothetical Novel"

Contents

1 ▪ Bulldog | 3

2 ▪ Rental House | 9

3 ▪ Small Wounds | 19

4 ▪ Fast Food | 35

5 ▪ Thieves | 45

6 ▪ Superfreak | 55

7 ▪ Mothers | 65

8 ▪ Love | 75

9 ▪ Term-Paper Topics | 81

10 ▪ Accidents | 89

11 ▪ Hunters | 95

12 ▪ In the Woods | 107

13 ▪ A Situation | 111

14 ▪ Break Up | 115

15 ▪ Fight | 119

16 ▪ Memory | 129

17 ▪ Family | 131

FIGHT SCENES

Bulldog

The dog had nearly hanged herself, in her maniacal aggression, from a stout oak tree. This was in 1983. Mark and I were twelve, a couple of what used to be called "at risk" kids. We stood outside the chain-link fence, in his father's narrow side-yard, watching.

Winter-brown grass crunched under our shoes. A jet from the nearby Air Force base, where my mother worked as a secretary, roared over us, writing a thick chalk line of exhaust across the sky.

We looked up, at each other, back at Bulldog balanced on her hind legs at the end of the taut leash, tongue out, hopping, gagging, her pink chest forward, exposed. She was short, bulky, white with large brown spots, one encircling her left eye. The leash was wrapped several times around the trunk. Every fourth or fifth inhale was a panicked, gasping snort, her breath pluming out like a cartoon dialogue bubble.

"I told you," Mark said, in that petulant, contorted-face way he had. His parents were in the middle of the divorce: name-calling, a custody battle (both parents wanted *visiting* rights). "She's insane. She does this every time she sees me. She bit someone in my mom's neighborhood, so my mom told my dad he had to keep her here until they could sell her. My mom says my dad drinks and that's why the dog is wild. She's like, 'Stop drinking and pay some attention to the dog.' And then he's like, 'I don't drink.' And then she's like, 'I can't talk to you. Why do you lie? Why do you lie? It's over and you're still lying.' I hate my parents, man. I wish my mom would die sometimes."

"Who's going to buy a dog like that?" I asked.

"She's a purebred." He put his chapped hand on the top bar of the fence, sending the barking noise up a decibel. "So you have to find like a dog person, you know, a purebred person, someone with money. My parents bought her when they were trying to keep everyone in one house. At least they didn't have a baby. Christ."

Bulldog's eyes bulged; her rage sent a tingle like someone's fingers across my scalp.

4

"Come on," Mark said. "Watch this." He went up and over the fence.

The dog became wilder, hopping much higher than before, baring her teeth, slobbering soapy foam. She was either going to strangle herself or get loose and tear him to shreds.

I climbed the fence, jumped. My new friend did it. I had to.

I landed, looked around, felt like I was inside a large cage. Dog feces everywhere. Even in the freezing weather the warm smell wafted, filled my nose and mouth. I gagged.

I stood fifteen feet or so from Bulldog, whose anger was a magnetic field. I felt it in my back and neck, heat down in my legs. I looked into her chopping mouth. I could hardly breathe.

Mark picked up a rusty hatchet from beside the wood-pile. "Come on!" he yelled at the dog. "Come on!"

He wound up, hand cocked high over his head. He threw it.

My whole body blinked. My hands curled like claws; my shoulders flinched up toward my ears ...

When I opened my eyes, Mark turned toward me, laughing, the hatchet still in his hand, a tormentor playing a joke for my enjoyment.

"You little bitch," he said. "You girl!"

Did the dog yelp and briefly cower? Could it show fear anymore? Or had that been lost by now?

I don't know. There's a black space here. My mind sees only Mark's face, and then the hatchet blade, brown with rust.

What I do remember clearly, what happened next—the image organizing these words, beginning this story—is how Bulldog went at him then, the feral, almost otherworldly sound of her, the way she pulled hard against the leash, stretching her leather and metal collar until it was about to break, willing, like the rest of them, to be hanged there by her own truculence if that's what it took to get revenge.

Rental House

The divorce final, Mark lived with his father in the small brick rental house at the swampy end of Black's Lake Road. He called his father Bill. I spent a lot of time that year at the house.

Bill was six-foot-two, maybe six foot-three, with curly brown hair thinning on top and puffing out like a clown's wig on the sides. A thick beard covered his face; he had coarse, black stubble on his neck and high cheekbones; muscles and veins rippled down his forearms, the tan part not covered by his sawdusted flannel shirts. He was a great dad, I thought for a time: the opposite of my own, who was serious and busy, who wondered where I was while he was at work and told me when to be home, who often asked me what he smelled on my breath.

Bill didn't seem concerned by anything at all. He let Mark do whatever he wanted. He laughed a lot and said, "Well, suck my peter," or "Well, spank my ass," in front of a group of twelve-year-olds who'd smack each other and laugh and repeat the phrase. When Mark and I shaved our heads down to stubble and started wearing T-shirts with the sleeves cut off—this was just weeks after Mark's mother left Bill to live with another woman and begin painting seascapes and dabbling in Wicca—he said, in the most somber tone I ever heard him use, "What the hell are y'all supposed to be? Fags?"

In every season but the short southeastern Virginia winter, Bill worked construction six days a week. A few of the men from his crew were often over at their house after work, drinking beer and smoking dope. I watched Bill drink five, six, seven beers some evenings as the smoky orange sun sank in their dusty bay window, down into the tops of dark houses and the black woods. He became funnier as the empty cans multiplied, more alive and animate. He held everyone's attention. I stared at his red face, the crease lines, the way he gesticulated with a Budweiser can: "So this chick . . ." he said. Or: "So this gal is at the bar and I . . ." He made me want to drink, to have command over women, to get good at all of it, to tell these kinds of stories, to be a man.

After drinking for a couple of hours, Bill and the men (I see a lot of different faces as I think of these men, not even faces, just features like beards and long hair and tanned, dried skin) went out to bars and strip clubs in Newport News. Mark and I then had the house to ourselves.

"My dad gets laid a lot," Mark said one night after the men had gone out in a breeze of laughter.

"No kidding," I said.

"He has these pictures." He got down on his knees and reached under the stained green couch. I thought he was going to pull out a photo album or a magazine (porn magazines were almost as numerous as dirty socks and underwear around the house). But he moved a full ashtray and some of the cans on the coffee table and put Bill's cookie sheet, covered in de-seeded pot, down upon it. "Pictures of this woman. I don't know who she is."

"Let me see," I said. "Where are they?"

He laid out a paper to roll a joint. He wasn't wearing a shirt, and his sternum stuck out of his pale boy's skin like an Adam's apple. "I don't know. It's weird." He paused, eyed what he was rolling. "Nah, I'm kidding. There aren't any pictures. I was making that up." He laughed. "I wanted to see if you'd believe me."

He often lied, for no good reason. By the time he moved away at sixteen, we didn't hang out anymore because he'd told so many lies I couldn't decipher who he was. He had black circles under his eyes from all the drugs, drinking. He looked twenty, twenty-three, twenty-five, with a wet eyebrow of a mustache over his lip, constellations of acne on his forehead and chin. He'd camouflaged himself in inebriation and deceit, but at twelve, on this day I'm telling you about, during this year I'm going to tell you about, he was still the coolest kid I knew, my best friend.

We smoked. I let it go.

Later, sitting on the couch with wet, red eyes, he said, "So you want to see the pictures?"

"Yeah." I wasn't sure what he was talking about. "Of the woman, you mean?"

"Yeah," he sneered. "What do you think?"

"You said you didn't have them, you made them up."

"I didn't say that. I said it was weird."

"You said you made them up."

"Faggot, do you want to see them or not?"

"I said yeah. That's what I said."

"You're acting like a dumb-ass. You're acting like Steve when he gets high. I shouldn't even show you. You'll probably start touching yourself."

"Man . . . ," I started to say. I felt anxious. Was I acting weird?

"They're my pictures."

"You said your dad's."

"They're mine because they're in my house ... Stop arguing with me so I can get them."

"That's what I'm saying."

At the other end of the house, in the back bedroom, in a green work-boot box under Bill's disheveled bed, were about twenty Polaroids of a naked blonde woman. Her hair was pulled back in some pictures, ponytailed in others, down and long and shining in the rest. The poses were from magazines, ritualistic—her sitting on a chair holding up her breasts, smiling; on all fours, ass in the air, eyes red from the flash; on a table with her knees apart, frozen in either a giggle or a grimace, her white skin corpse-like. My heart— I'll have to use a cliché here—*raced*. I felt hot, sick. The air shone around us yellow and dirty, almost oily; I would have sworn there was a faint buzzing coming through me from every electronic gadget in the house.

At the moment, as I looked at the pictures, she seemed old, like someone's beautiful mom. Years later, as a man, a father of daughters, remembering this: She was twenty, twenty-one; a dancer, some junior college girl from a local bar, someone's daughter who woke up the next morning thinking, *What did I do?* I see her, in a way, every time I go back to the sprawling suburbs where I grew up. She drives an older Pontiac, or a Chevrolet, sometimes a foreign compact, and there are three, four, five kids in the car, a couple of them her sister's or a friend's; she looks tired; she and her second husband have split because there was just no love there, none at all, and she's not alive to be insulted (I start writing a story about her in my head as I drive by her). She thinks (because she has become who she is): *I'm heavier than I would like to be. My hair needs something in it—color, or layers. That will really do it.* She's headed to an ATM, the gas station, the grocery store, the movie rental place. She can't believe the traffic. The kids want something, need something: "Mom!"

Mark and I sat on Bill's unmade bed, staring at her—her skin, nipples, dark eyes, mouth.

"Mark," I said. "This is so cool."

Mark's face, thin and a little scowling naturally, clenched and hardened. He was stoned, and he'd had a beer, too. A good idea, to show these pictures, to invade Bill's bedroom, but the reality of it quickly soured. Suddenly he looked as if he might cry, run out of the room. I wasn't used to him like this.

"Maybe they aren't your dad's," I said. I realized, or thought I realized, that the pictures, the idea of his dad and this woman, brought up visions of his mom, how everything—their family, the happiness I'm sure they once had—was over for good. (It's like this: You're twelve, angry, sad, and lost; you get high: barriers come down; you float in and out of the painful parts of your past, get stuck in some dark room in the back of your developing, drugged brain and then the door gets locked and the devil's stereo is on and all the songs are about divorce and lying and how tiring it is to hate all the time, how that kind of thing burns a little ulcer in your soul.) I went on, trying to cheer him up: "They could belong to one of the guys. They're probably Rusty's." Rusty was a roofer who always hung around. He'd been arrested for drunk driving a couple of times, talked about fighting in bars. A lot of his stories headed toward the phrase "and then I decked the guy." He told Mark and me about getting the clap, how it burned when you took a leak. He told us, back in the winter, that he'd "had more pussy than we'd ever get in our life, combined." He showed us a porn film once—or rather watched one without telling us to leave the room—and that was how I found out that something *came out of you* when you had sex, which was alarming.

"Yeah," Mark said, looking up, half-smiling. "They have to be Rusty's. My dad . . . he's just keeping them here because Rusty's always moving to some new apartment. Or getting kicked out of some place."

"Yeah," I assured him. "They're Rusty's. This is something Rusty would do."

"I mean, my dad and my mom talk sometimes. On the phone." He held up a Polaroid. "I don't even know who this slut is."

I nodded. Situation rationalized—she meant nothing—we spread the pictures out on the bed. Our eyes moved over her.

"Let's take a picture out to the fort," Mark said. We had some weathered, spray-painted plywood nailed into walls and a roof between trees in the copse of woods beside his house. In the middle of the fort was a hole with a small, metal box in it, covered over by another small piece of plywood. We kept shop-class-carved pot pipes and a lighter and a bottle opener in the box. Occasionally we had liquor, or a warm beer or two, or packs of half-crushed cigarettes.

"I don't think anyone would miss one picture," I said. "I think we could take one picture."

Mark put one of the all-fours shots, but not the best one, in the back pocket of his jeans. We put the rest back in the box, and I pushed it under the bed.

We went to the fort, out into the last sunlight blinking through the fingers of the trees; we pushed leaves, vines, sank into the evening. The earth was dusk-gray and dry and light as talcum as we ducked, leaned, stepped over hacked stumps.

"Let's fuck her," Mark said in the fort. He sat in the dirt, cross-legged, his face shadowy in the bluing light, his white T-shirt nearly glowing.

"Who?" I said.

He leaned forward and pulled the picture out of his

16

pocket. It was a little crumpled, the photo surface like a spider-cracked windshield. Dirt from his hands stained the white edges. "Her."

"What are you *talking* about?"

"Let's take her into the woods and both of us can do it." He was serious.

I looked at him, the photo. "It's a *picture*," I said.

He looked down, studied her. There was a long pause. He looked at me, my mocking face, and thought for a second. "I'm just kidding, man. I'm not *gay*. I'm not like a pervert or something." He pushed my shoulder. "I definitely don't want to see your little boner."

It was late. I needed to get home. Every time I smoked pot, something strange happened to the language coming out of people's faces. "I'll see you tomorrow, dude. My dad."

As I walked down the narrow path, back toward the yard, Mark yelled, "Look!"

I turned around. Through the dark I saw a small wiggling flame in the air. I could just make out the shape of Mark beside it. He'd gotten the lighter from the box in the fort, and now he held the burning photo by one corner. "I'm killing her! I'm killing her!" He let out a loud laugh. Then in a high-pitched voice: "Oh help me help me help me. I'm a whore. I'm *dyyyying*." He dropped the picture and pounded out the flames with his sneakered foot.

I turned back around, shook my head, and started walking. All over my childhood are these memories to walk away from.

"*Hey*," he said sharply.

I stopped. "What?"

"Don't tell anyone about the pictures under my dad's bed, OK?"

"Shut up," I said. "I won't."

Small Wounds

One day I walked to a girl's house to have my first kiss. Her name was Hazel. She was known as the school slut.

Hazel had the body of a woman—big hips, large chest, legs thick and long and healthy. She was inhuman to my friends and to me, more a three-dimensional picture drifting down lockered hallways, a thing built for sexual experiment, than a person with a life, a history, feelings. I remember her dark hair and round cheeks, her deep-set blue eyes, each one encircled by a faint bruising I now associate with sleeplessness, with the mind rattling intense and directionless at all hours.

"She'll do stuff," Mark had said, walking along the sidewalk, under humming power lines, past the white and blue and green vinyl-sided, two-story houses of our suburb. "My mom babysat her and her sister when we were kids. Plus her old boyfriend—you know that guy Clark with the mustache?—used to do her every day after school. Before him her boyfriend was like thirty. And that guy's in *jail*."

Standing on Hazel's porch, Mark peered through the front window. He brushed past me and rang the doorbell. I tried to believe only some of what he said. He took a couple of his mother's old diet pills some mornings and prattled on unstoppable.

Hazel lived in a nice house—brick, big for that neighborhood. Everywhere in her yard were flowers, surrounded by perfectly manicured mulch beds. I had a momentary feeling of walking into a half-remembered dream about a graveyard, people popping out of the ground with flowers in their hair. There were no cars in the driveway. No traffic on the street. Mark rang again. We waited, but no one came.

"Come on," he said. We walked around the house and into a back door. I'd known Mark for about a year at this point, something like that, but I'd rarely heard him speak of Hazel, so it surprised me that he knew her well enough to walk into her empty house.

We sat down a cushion apart in a room with two couches arranged to face a big-screen TV. The house was dark and air-conditioned. I was amazed by the size of the TV. I'd never seen one so big.

"Menudo," Mark said, smiling and pointing at a poster on the wall of smooth, posing Latin boys.

I looked at the poster. He gave me a stare, pointed again. I scoffed. "Menudo sucks," I said. "They take it hard."

"Fags," he said.

"Spics," I said.

In one corner of the room were several stuffed unicorns of different colors. There was a box full of My Little Ponies— pink, blue, purple. I wondered where Hazel's underwear drawer was. I had recently seen a late movie on cable about a peeping tom, the peeping tom rendered somehow sympathetic, and intriguing, by the director. I spent a lot of time imagining myself as someone else, trying on, in the course of a day or even a few hours, several identities. My sweaty legs stuck to the leather couch. I could see myself hiding in dark bushes, staring into glowing windows.

"What are you doing?" Hazel said half an hour later, walking in the back door, into the room. Hot, bright air rushed in behind her. She was wearing jean shorts, a light-blue T-shirt with a rainbow and butterfly screen-printed on it, and flip-flops.

"Watching cable," Mark said. On the screen a lone, good cop battled Nazi skinheads in California who were throwing trashcans off overpasses onto the cars of blond, innocent families going on vacations, singing campfire songs.

Hazel looked at me. I smiled. I felt the day's heat pass through me. She made an annoyed face. I looked down.

"Who's he?" she said.

Mark said my name.

"He's ugly."

I didn't look anywhere but where I was looking. I don't think my face changed at all, but my ego had been dismembered and crammed into a trunk.

"I didn't say you could be in my house," she said to Mark. "Why do you think it's OK to walk into people's houses?"

A shorter, lighter version of Hazel walked in then. "Hi, Mark," she said.

"Hi, Sissy."

"Don't say, 'Hi, Mark,'" Hazel said. "He just walked into our house. I could call the cops. I could call Dad."

"You're dramatic," Sissy said.

"I'm serious," Hazel said.

"Who are you?" Sissy said, noticing me.

I didn't say anything. I worried about how my face would look, how I might be exposed if I tried to move my mouth enough to push words out.

Mark said my name again. "You know his brother, I think."

"Oh, yeah," she said. "Your brother is way fucked. What a fucking nut job Jesus freak. How much acid has he taken?"

I shrugged.

"So you don't talk?"

"I talk," I said.

Sissy looked at me and let out a cackle.

"Isn't he ugly?" Hazel said. "Your crazy brother isn't that ugly, but you're really disgusting. I wonder how that happened. Is one of your parents ugly?"

"I don't think he's ugly," Sissy said. "Punk is over. Let your hair grow. That would help. Didn't you like have a shag or a bi-level last year? Weren't you like a member of KISS for Halloween? Peter Chris or Ace Freeley?"

"You have no taste," Hazel said to Sissy.

"Oh, God. Shut up, cellulite ass!"

"At least my pussy doesn't smell."

"Like roses."

"Like *dis*ease."

"Bitch."

"Cunt."

"Your momma."

"Yours."

I'd never heard girls talk like this; females were a mystery, like Eskimos or movie stars. The girls walked upstairs, out of the game room, or the TV room, or the den, or whatever it was, and into the kitchen. Mark motioned for me to come on. I followed Mark following the girls, confused about how getting kicked out had become an invitation.

We drank vodka from Hazel's father's liquor cabinet. Her father had drawn a faint line on the bottle's label. Hazel refilled the bottle with water exactly to the line.

After drinking about a quarter of the bottle between us, half a coffee cup of straight vodka each, the day warped a little. I wasn't drunk, but the world was looser and less serious. I shed embarrassment and shame; my ego pieced itself back together. I probably fell in love with alcohol, wonderful and soul-numbing, on this very day.

Mark and Sissy went into a back bedroom. There was no working up to this, no flirting, no preteen foreplay. They just stood up, looked at each other, and walked back there.

I sat at the kitchen table with Hazel. My face felt big and my stomach made an odd plumbing sort of noise. The faucet dripped every ten seconds or so, one *bloop*. The AC kicked on, and a blue-flowered drape waved like the hem of a dress. I could see the reflections of my arms under my arms in the polished wood.

"Do you want to arm wrestle?" she said. "I bet I could beat you."

She was a head taller than me, and two years older. She looked strong. "Nah," I said.

"You're scared." Her words were just perceptibly slurred, slipping over the "s."

"No, I'm not," I said.

I was surprised to beat her four times in a row.

"Let's wrestle," she said. "My arms are too long to arm wrestle. You have short arms, so that's why you win. You're sort of trollish. You're kind of like a tall midget—a tall midget with bad hair." She snorted.

I said I was going downstairs to wait for Mark. There was no way for something like this to turn out well.

She followed me down and turned off the TV as soon as I clicked it on and sat down. "I didn't say you could watch my TV."

"OK," I said. "I'll go."

"Yeah. Go. You have horrible breath. And nice haircut, faggot. You look like Freddy Mercury. Like where's your leotard?"

I stood up, looking toward the back door. She laughed and pushed me. Then we were standing face to face in front of the TV. The TV was so big that from a certain angle we would have looked like two characters projected out of it.

"Don't push me." I tried on nonchalant.

"Come on," she said, pushing me again. "Wrestle me."

I stepped back, put my hands up, flashed a diffusing smile. "I'll wait outside."

She grabbed my arm. I was buzzed, and it happened quickly—a hot, sharp surge. I looked down at five red sickle moons in my forearm. Blood pooled in the deepest mark, made by her thumb.

"You think you can come over here and be with me!" she yelled. I was still looking at my arm and stepped back to keep my face from getting raked. "You can come over here and do what you want with me?"

She sat on the couch, as if she was suddenly exhausted, and put her head in her hands, very dramatically. "You don't know me," she said. Then she looked up, at the room, at me, her eyes soot-dark and glistening. "You don't know me. You don't know anything about me."

"Look," I said. "I just came over here with Mark. Mark wanted to come over here."

She wiped at one eye. "He didn't say *anything* about me?"

"No. Nothing. Well, he said that his mother babysat you a long time ago."

She tilted her head.

"I'm not lying," I said.

"I didn't mean to scratch you. That was totally an accident. You hate me now, don't you?"

"Not really."

"Yes, you do."

"No, I don't."

"You do. I don't blame you. You should hate me. I mean, you should. Everyone hates me. Even my dad."

"I don't."

"Sit down with me."

I held my arm.

"Please."

I sat on the cushion beside her but leaned away, still holding my arm, though it wasn't bleeding badly, just spotty around the marks. A square of sunlight from the window was on the floor beside us.

"You can hold me if you want. But don't be a perv."

I looked at her face. She had small pimples, blackheads, around her mouth. Her breath smelled faintly of Italian salad dressing. I'd never been so close to such beauty, such raw, messy beauty. I rested my bloody arm against her back.

"You're not that ugly," she said. "It's just that I don't like your type. Your type is usually very annoying to me."

"I like being ugly," I lied. "Johnny Rotten is ugly. Joe Strummer is ugly."

"Don't you want to kiss?" she said.

"OK."

We kissed for several minutes, awkwardly at first, clicking teeth, pushing tongues against closed lips, breathing too loudly through our noses, but she showed me how to slow down, to get lost in the moment—she knew how to do

27

this—and I did, I got lost, became only tongue and lips and cumbersome teeth.

Then she had to go to the bathroom.

She came back holding a magazine and sat down against me, putting her head on my shoulder, laying the magazine in my lap.

A naked man and woman were touching tongues on the front.

"Open it," she said.

I opened it.

"It's my father's. He uses it for masturbation." She looked at me. Her face was just inches from mine and I wanted to kiss her again—that word. "You know, jerking off?"

"I know what it means."

"Well you had a blank look. Go on, flip through."

I flipped through. It was—so to speak—the story of a grocery delivery boy (although he looked thirty or so) and a lonely, gorgeous housewife who vacuumed her opulent house wearing a black negligee.

"Look at that," she said. "Have you seen . . . My God!"

We laughed. I kissed her, just grazed her, desperate, but she pushed me away. She was done kissing now.

"Come on," she said, jumping up. "Let's go out back. I want to show you something."

I had to adjust myself as she turned and walked out the

back door. There was a warm humming way down in my stomach. I felt heavier, not in control of my body.

Out back, under a bright summer sun, there were even more flowers. Beds and beds. And someone had taken the time to plant them in patterns, I now noticed—one bed was purple, white, purple, white; another red, orange, pink, yellow, red, orange, pink, yellow. It was like a garden center, or something you'd see in a magazine.

"These are mine," she said. "I did all this."

"Wow," was all I could think to say.

Birds wheeled over us. Some hopped along the ground. Bees hovered and dipped all around. The atmosphere was ridiculous.

She explained every flower to me. She had my blood on the back of her shirt. It took her an hour or more of fast-talking: here's how I did this; here's why I chose these. She knew all the biological terms. She knew botanical history.

We sat on an iron bench she had bought with her own money to put out among her flowers.

"Do you ever think of offing yourself?" she said.

"Yes," I said, though I hadn't at that point, was just lying to make conversation. "I think of it all the time."

"I think of it all the time, too." A bird hopped along in the grass in front of us. "Especially when I come out here. I think sometimes that I should eat a bottle of pills and chase them with vodka and then come out here, in my flowers, and die. Or I could cut both of my wrists—cut them the long way, and deep—and walk out here dripping blood all over the flowers, all across the flowers, leaving a red trail out to the place where my dad would eventually find my body. I'd wear my favorite dress. There would be birds all around me. There would be flies buzzing around the wounds in my wrists." She laughed.

"That's horrible," I said. "A sad thought."

"But I'm not going to do it."

"Good."

"Do you want to know why?" she said.

"I'm just glad you're not going to kill yourself," I said. "I mean, think of your dad finding you dead in all these flowers."

"Well, I'll tell you why. Because I want to have babies. I want to be a mother. I'd like to have maybe five babies and then adopt a couple more."

"You'll be really busy," I said.

"I know I will," she said, excited, touching my hand and sending a jolt through me. "I know. I'm going to hold each one of them, you know, and cuddle them, and let them sleep in the bed with my husband and me. Every day when I wake up I'm going to tell each one of them how much I love them—I mean I'm going to say it *every single day*—and when I give them baths at night, when I'm drying them off, you know, I'm going to kiss their little feet and hands. I'm going to sniff their hair and tickle them. I want them to laugh a lot."

"Wow," I said. "That sounds great. I'm totally happy for your kids. I bet they'll do interesting things when they grow up."

Just then Mark came out back. He shouted my name and waved. He started walking away fast. I told Hazel I'd better go with him. I ran to catch up.

"Bye," she yelled. I looked back and smiled. "I liked talking to you."

Out on the street, heading home, Mark was quiet, his teeth clenched. A school bus groaned by. Several of the kids in the back, a Little League baseball team, flipped us off. Mark didn't even flip them off or grab his crotch in response.

I put up a middle finger. "Fuck off!" I shouted. Then to Mark: "What's wrong with you?"

He kept walking. Finally, after maybe a minute, he said, "That bitch Sissy is a tease. She's a total dyke. A muff-diver, dude. I'm going to write that she's a dyke in every bathroom at school. A turbo-diesel dyke!"

We walked on. I let him fume away. What did I care? I was thinking of kissing Hazel, of her father's magazine, of lonely, sexy people waiting for someone, anyone, to drop

GREG BOTTOMS

by. My mind was filled with colorful flowers and death and babies and my blood drying on a beautiful girl's shirt.

"What about you?" he finally said. "Did you get anything?"

I couldn't think of what to say. There was too much to say, and I was unable then to give shape or meaning to any of it. I held out my bloody arm as if to explain.

Fast Food

The backseat of Rusty's red Chevelle smelled of mildewed work shirts. They lay heaped in sweat-damp balls on the floor. There were also hints of body odor, fast food, coffee, and alcohol-sick flatulence: fermented fruit, campground outhouse. Mark and I sat on the cracked black upholstery, among wrappers and cups, because Rusty—his stringy brown hair now flapping in the wind—said only grown-ups and pussy could ride up front. I looked out the window, blinking in the warm wind, as we sped past convenience stores and new construction fencing, headed to Popeye's Chicken & Biscuits.

Bill had given Rusty five dollars to buy dinner for Mark

because he'd be out all night with a woman he'd met at a bar. Since Rusty was now living with Bill and Mark for free after getting kicked out of his apartment, Bill sometimes asked him to do what Rusty called "babysitting favors," like getting Mark food or dropping him off at school. I was tagging along, as usual.

"I don't like Popeye's," Mark said. "The chicken has weird spices in it. Go to McDonald's."

"Forget McDonald's, man," Rusty said, as if Ronald McDonald had personally done something to him. "They don't have Pepsi."

"So *what*," Mark said. "You're always talking about Pepsi. You should *work* for Pepsi. All the cans you leave around the house." Mark was right—since Rusty had moved in, Pepsi cans covered their kitchen counter, lay crumpled in the smoky den, and filled up their trashcan, a giant green outdoor bin sitting, fetid and sticky, by the rusty-handled refrigerator.

"You don't like the cans," Rusty said, "pick them up. Your dad gives you allowance, don't he? You sure don't earn it."

"I cut the grass," Mark said.

"If that's what you call leaving patches and islands all over the yard. My daddy would have beaten me with a stick if I cut grass like you. He'd have picked up the biggest thing near-to-hand and cracked me in the head."

"Whatever," Mark said. "You know everything. I'm sure you're like a professional lawn-care person, too."

"No, I'm a damn *baby*sitter."

"Not my babysitter," Mark said, huffing and looking out the window.

Five minutes later Mark said, "Popeye's is nigger food, man. I can't believe you like it. All you talk about is how lazy the black guys on your crew are and then you go and buy their food."

"Popeye's is country cooking," Rusty said. "Popeye's, for your info, was started by a white man in New Orleans."

"Like you know."

"I do know, smart mouth. I read something somewhere. A magazine article."

"Oh, yeah," Mark said. "I've seen how you like to sit around reading magazines."

He and I laughed.

"Shut your damn smart mouth," Rusty said, his tone more tired than angry. "If you weren't Bill's son . . ."

We pulled into the Popeye's parking lot. Summer storm clouds roiled above. There was a commotion on the sidewalk out front. We blurred past it—color and crazed movement.

I looked back. A white guy with cropped black hair, wearing a thin Army jacket, was screaming at someone in a car backing out of a parking space.

We parked. When Rusty cut the engine, I heard the guy shout, "I'll stick you. I'll take a syringe and stick you!"

Once out of the car, I hesitated, standing by the door. Homeless people drifted around these rougher neighborhoods in Newport News. Not long before this a kid named Shackleton, a thirteen-year-old with a cousin-inflicted tattoo and holes in his clothes, had pulled a large hunting knife on me (I threw a plastic cafeteria chair at him and ran), and one of my older brother's former dope friends, in the spring, had tripped me backward, knees over head over knees, into a cold, muddy, steep-sided creek, which I had a hard time climbing out of, churning my feet in place, sliding down. I'd learned to be careful, to avoid contact with certain people. I waited for Rusty, who was putting on his T-shirt.

Rusty was about six feet tall, bulky, with a tan, hairless, thick belly, a horizontal crease across his navel like a frown. He also had a permanent white indentation on one hip from his tool belt. His arms were meaty and hard from carrying the shingle bundles he used in his roofing work.

"What's up?" Rusty said in a friendly voice to the screaming guy, who was puffed up with anger, almost glowing with it, as we walked past him, Mark and I staying close to Rusty.

"I don't know what's up," Screaming Guy said, sarcastically, face red, arms out like a preacher making a point. "I don't *know* what's up."

"OK, man," Rusty said. "OK. That's cool."

Inside, Popeye's was almost empty—a black elderly couple in one corner, a white teen in another corner. It was a little before dinnertime, maybe 4:30. I had to be home by six, when my mom returned from work.

I looked back through the glass doors to see Screaming Guy light a cigarette. Mark and Rusty looked, too, but carefully, with sideways glances, so he didn't think we were staring at him.

A few minutes later, the rain started. Screaming Guy came in, shaking the water out of his hair, brushing drops from his jacket. Rusty and Mark ate their two-piece chicken dinners by the window on the other side of the restaurant, as far away from Screaming Guy as we could get. I just sat with them (no money from Mom).

A very slim black teenage employee, seventeen or eighteen, was mopping the brown-tile floor in front of the cash registers. The floor was shiny and reflective behind her.

Screaming Guy stopped beside her, looked down at the top of her head. "Just what they need," he said in a loud voice. "Another little spook to do their dirty work."

She looked up. She had no expression at all, the way a person's face might look a split second before a car hit her.

We stared.

The elderly couple and the teenager stopped eating.

Total silence, save for the *tink-ta-tink-tink* of rain outside, the muffled rush of traffic as it rolled under billboards and up onramps.

Just as Screaming Guy was about to begin shouting, Rusty stood up and said, "Hey, hoss, hey, hoss," as he walked toward the two of them.

The teenager was in shock, it seemed, quiet. I imagine later she thought of all the things she could have said. She looked wiry and tough, and I bet she felt glum about letting something like that go, something so degrading and humiliating, but I was there, in the place, in the moment, and it was still possible that Screaming Guy was going to open his coat and cut us all down with automatic fire.

A couple of other workers, also black, came forward from the kitchen and stood behind the counter, watching, wondering what to do. Maybe they were thinking about calling the cops, I thought then, but years later, after I'd been broke a couple of times, and after I'd lived beside a halfway house on the edge of a ghetto for a couple of years, I learned firsthand that a lot of people in America don't immediately think to call the cops—think of cops as a last resort, people to avoid, just like, or sometimes worse than, criminals.

Screaming Guy bent his knees a little, ready to fight, when Rusty got to him.

"Hoss," Rusty said in an easy voice. "Come on now. Easy,

fella. I'm a friend. I'm a friend. You got to settle down. You're going to get the fuzz up in here, handcuffing people."

Screaming Guy looked hard at Rusty. His bangs were cut at a sharp, diagonal angle. His beard was patchy, black with some gray in it. His face was wet. His teeth were the color of old sidewalks.

"Can I get you a Pepsi?" Rusty said. "When I'm feeling down I have me a Pepsi and things start looking up. How about a biscuit, too? Popeye's has the best biscuits in the world, hoss. And cold Pepsi. A biscuit and a Pepsi. That's going to get us right. I think it is."

The teenager shook her head, took her mop, and quietly moved toward the kitchen.

Screaming Guy hesitated. There was a dark bruise on his temple, like a wine stain. "Alright," he said. His voice was scratchy from shouting and threatening people. "I'm pretty hungry."

"Then let's get a biscuit, hoss," said Rusty, patting him—a risky move—on the back.

I could see that one of the two guys working was amping up to give Screaming Guy a piece of his mind. But at the counter Rusty made an easy, waving gesture with his hand, which Screaming Guy didn't see, to let the workers know that everything was under control. Everything was going to be cool.

Sitting down with us, Screaming Guy smelled metallic and rusty, like blood and a popped battery. As menacing as he was, the scent he gave off made me think of the losing side of violence—adrenaline and fear. He was deathly afraid of something, of airplanes dropping bombs on him, of God poking his hand out of the sky and pointing a finger at him so everyone would finally *know*, of his mother's ravaged ghost walking out of the woods of the city park, where drug users and gay teens communed around the filthy public restrooms. He was a rat, cornered and baring his teeth.

He sat beside Rusty, across from me, eating and talking. What he was trying to say was jumbled, wind and sound and biscuit crumbs leaving a mouth. But then he got going about knots for a while, how he could tie a rolling hitch and a slippery hitch and a mooring hitch, how he grew up in downtown Hampton, the next city over, in the Phoebus section, a poor section, where my father grew up, right on the water, how his daddy had a boat and used to take him crabbing, how there were fewer crabs now, how you couldn't make a living.

Then he mentioned the Coast Guard recruiting office. "Some *nigger*," he said, and the word just took a lap around the room, "is going to tell me I'm unfit for service? Is going to tell me I've failed some bullshit test?"

The elderly couple was frozen in place. The white teen got up, slowly, to leave.

"Whoa, hoss," Rusty said, glancing around. "Let's keep our voices down. Let's not get to shouting and insulting."

"I can shout if I want!"

"Hoss hoss hoss hoss," Rusty said. "I've got the way for you to fix all this." Screaming Guy looked at Rusty. Mark looked at Rusty. I looked at Rusty. "But you've got to settle down," Rusty went on. "This is a public restaurant. I hear what you're saying. But we've got to keep it down."

Screaming Guy grabbed the edges of the orange, plastic table. "Tell me," he said, sounding like a mad five-year-old. "Tell me. Tell me. What am I going to do?"

"I'll tell you. I'm going to tell you," Rusty said. "When you're calm. Go on and have a drink of Pepsi. Get straight."

Mark and I waited, listening.

Rusty leaned forward. Screaming Guy leaned forward. "You go down to the Coast Guard recruiting office," Rusty said in a low voice, almost a whisper, looking around, "and you ask to talk to one of the *white* recruiters. I believe"— Rusty winked—"things will come out better. I reckon they'll have you on a boat by month's end, hoss."

Screaming Guy sat up straight and wrinkled his forehead, which was more exposed on one side than the other because of his chopped haircut.

In the parking lot, back in the car, Mark said, "What the hell? Way to invite Frankenstein to eat with us, man."

GREG BOTTOMS

Rusty cranked the engine. "That guy was harmless," he said. "I got ten dudes on my crew that ain't much better off than him—talk about blacks like the Klan, sit fifty yards away from them at lunch break. He's just some redneck who's done drunk himself loony. Hell, a white Coast Guard officer is liable to lock his ass in the brig until the paddy wagon shows up with the straightjacket."

As Rusty talked, I could still see Screaming Guy walking away—the back of his army jacket, his cropped hair, his loping shuffle—but I had a dreamy, detached feeling, a floating feeling, as if all that had just happened was imagined, happened in some alternate universe and was witnessed by a character both me and not quite me.

Rusty beeped the Chevelle's horn and waved when we drove past Screaming Guy on our way home. I turned around and looked at him through the back window. Raindrops slid down the glass between us. I kept looking until the drops were bigger than he was, big enough to drown him. Then he was gone.

Thieves

Much of my life has been a daydream, a here-but-not-here experience. In 1983, as I'm remembering and re-creating it, these daydreams could roll over me like a tide. I'd forget myself and become part of the summer day with its haze and stillness, float slowly past the insect-singing trees, the sulfur-smelling creek sizzling in the sun, past the 7-Eleven and the strip mall and the car dealership (BIG JULY 4TH SALE—BUY AMERICAN), into the woods and out of the woods and into the woods again, then through the glassless front window of the apartment building being built in the next neighborhood over and out of the back opening where a sliding-glass door would one day be, landing in the churned-up, bulldozer-tracked dirt and stepping—*boom*—back into the flow of time.

I'd go looking for something to do.

One Saturday morning a woman wearing nothing but one of Bill's T-shirts stood in the driveway of the brick rental house. She didn't see me walking toward her because she was staring through the passenger-side window of a 1970s blue Ford Mustang. It had rust spots along the edges of the fenders, on the back bumper.

I stopped and looked down to make sure I wasn't hovering.

"*Man*," the woman said. She had bed-head, shoulder-length brown hair and a sleep-softened face. Her legs were long and fit, her breasts large and loose inside the T-shirt. I could see the shape of her nipples in the cotton, like pencil erasers or spitballs.

"What the hell?" she said, seeing me now as I stood stupidly in the scorched street.

"Mark here?" I asked, before she could chastise me for staring at her while she wasn't looking.

Mark creaked open the front screen door, let it slam behind him. "Hey, idiot," he said, jumping off the stoop, over the tall grass that grew high up against it. "I got this coat hanger we can bend," he said to the woman. He looked at me. "We got a problem. We got a huge problem, man."

"Yeah," I said, though I had no idea what anyone was talking about. I assumed—and this could generally describe my childhood—that if I kept participating things would somehow become clear.

"Well, come on," she said, pointing toward the car. "I got the baby. Come on. It's me and the baby today."

Bill came out next—*creak, slam*—wearing tight gym shorts and a pair of unlaced, sand-colored work boots, the tongues flopped forward. He was hairy-chested and muscled. He looked like Tom Selleck in *Magnum PI*—one of my favorite shows that year—if you sent Selleck into the forest on some kind of peyote-taking vision quest for a couple of weeks.

"I got to get going," the woman said, a note of panic in her voice. "I got to get going." She said "going" like my grandmother, who was from the flat farmlands of eastern North Carolina, like "go-in": "I gotta git go-in."

Bill said, "We'll do this. I'm a lover and a car thief, baby. Right here with the hanger, Mark. I'm Steve McQueen. I'm Steve McQueen." He mimicked an action-movie guitar riff with his mouth and quickly humped the air with a couple of hip pumps.

We all lined up and looked into the car, which was about 120 degrees inside, I'd guess. A set of keys hung from the ignition. The seats were blue pleather. There was a baby seat in the back. If there had been a baby, it would have been roasting by now. I thought about what I'd need to do—the emergency plan—if there was a baby inside. After a second, I decided I'd take a mossy cinderblock from beside the garage and smash the windshield, hoping that no shards of glass hit the baby, though certainly some would, so I'd have to contend with those injuries as well as the screaming and possible vomiting. The baby would be crying, panicked, so I'd have to work fast, jumping onto the hood, mustering . . .

"*Man*," the woman said again.

Bill said, "Don't worry."

Mark swatted a mosquito on his neck.

The car, the heat, the bugs, the daydreaming—we were all lost for a minute. If you were above us, I mean way above us, looking down, you might have offered us your pity.

"Alright. Look out." Bill started bending a small loop into one end of the now straightened-out hanger.

"Who drove?" the woman said, running her fingers through her hair. "I don't remember. Did I drive, Bill? I've already got a drunk driving from once a while ago back aways like last year."

Bill slid the hanger between the rubber seal of the door and the glass. He was contorting himself, doing a kind of pool-hall body English, as he turned it so the loop would lasso the passenger-side door lock. He stopped what he was doing and looked at her. "You drove, honey," he said quietly. Pause. Faster, louder: "Yeah. You couldn't wait to get here. You were *speeding*, if you know what I mean." He kept staring at her, waiting for her reply.

"Well, I don't know," she said after a moment. She looked at each of us and then down at herself. She crossed her arms, suddenly noticing the fact that she was only wearing a man's T-shirt, was almost naked in a front yard, in a suburban neighborhood. She looked at the weather-scarred house across the street, the door-less car on its wild lawn, the blue-tick hound in a circle of dirt and a pool of tree shade, its back against the cool of the chain-link fence. I could see now that her sleep-softened glow was really a half-conscious hangover. She went, in a matter of seconds, from being glorious to seeming like the victim of a minor accident.

Bill kept at the lock.

The day's brightness had orders to incinerate us.

"This can't be happening," the woman said half an hour later, when it was clear the unlocking wasn't going to be easy. "Momma doesn't even get up until noon. She doesn't know the routine. She doesn't know how to do breakfast or get Alex ready for the sitter and she should be already at the sitter's. I can't believe I drove. *I* drove? Alex is up. I know she is. Should call, but Jesus, I don't want to call and hear all about it if Momma answers with a crying toddler and wants to start talking at me like I ain't a grown-up cause she wasn't no prizewinner herself, I can tell you that much. I'm going to go out, you know what I mean. Or . . ." She looked at Bill's back, at Mark and me. "I need to go in and use your phone, Bill. I'll be back. Are you getting it? I'll be back. You gotta get it. Come on, McQueen. Help me out here."

The temperature was climbing through the mid-nineties. Bill sweated, beads like blisters on his skin, concentrating on the metal lasso and the Mustang's door lock.

He stopped what he was doing and looked at Mark and me once the screen door slammed behind the woman. "Jesus," he said. "She don't even remember who drove. I could have told her we came here in a police chopper." The lasso slipped off the lock as he talked. He cursed, went back to work on it.

Mark looked like he was going to say something. He had on a pair of flip-flops and blue corduroy Ocean Pacific shorts, which every cool kid wore back then. His arms were crossed. He shook his head, did a little annoyed roll of his eyes. "She's a prostitute, man," he said quietly. "Some kind of gutter slut."

"*Hey*," Bill said, stopping what he was doing, looking hard at Mark. "Watch your mouth, boy." He looked toward the house, back at Mark. In a low voice: "Watch your mouth. Don't be rude at my house. This girl ain't half-terrible."

A few minutes later Bill finally got the lasso securely on the lock, pulling it up with a *pop*. "I—am—good," he yelled. "I'm a car thief. I got a future." He did the mouth guitar riff and had his way with the air again. He pulled the hanger out, wiggling it past the window top, then straightened up, tall and muscled, and stretched his back and arms, which gave off a few *clicks* and *cracks*. Then he got in the car to unlock the other door. Whenever I saw him, when I really looked at him, which I only did if he was looking away, I stared at his muscles, the way his skin moved over them.

Hearing Bill, the woman hurried out—*creak, slam*—dressed in a denim miniskirt and a white blouse. "Well, I got her on the phone and she's in tears. Been calling around to the hospitals." She carried white hoop earrings around one wrist and red high-heeled shoes in the other hand. She toe-walked quickly through the grass and weeds and dandelions. This heat, the stretch of her shirt, her hair quickly combed: She really was beautiful.

"I got it," Bill said, waving the hanger. "Popped it like a pro."

"Oh, thank you," she said. "Thank the Lord. Thank the sweet Lord Jesus. I need a cigarette. I would kill a puppy, man, for a cigarette." She stopped on her way around to the driver's side, looked at Bill—not because she wanted to, or I don't think so anyway, but because it seemed like the only thing to do after waking up in a stranger's bed. "I, I had a good time," she said. "I had, you know, a real good time and all."

"You did," Bill said. He smiled. "We did, I mean. We surely did."

She looked at Bill's sweaty face, probably really seeing it for the first time, then tentatively got up on tiptoes and kissed him, just barely, on his bearded cheek.

When she had driven off, turned the Mustang around the corner down the block and was gone, Bill looked at Mark, who was still standing by the driveway, arms crossed. "What are you sulking about, boy?" he said. "Don't give me a rash. Don't do it. I'm telling you, do—not—do—it. You can go live with your mom if that's the way it's going to be. Thirteen years with one woman. She did the leaving. I'm a free man."

Mark stayed where he was.

Bill walked toward the house, then stopped and turned around, putting his hands up. "Come on," he said. He looked around the yard, as if what he needed to say to his son was out there. "Let's go get breakfast. Go to IHOP. I need a cup of coffee. I'll buy your buddy here breakfast, too. What's your name again?"

I told him my name.

"I'll buy you breakfast, too," he said, smiling.

As Mark walked past him, Bill grabbed him in a headlock and squeezed his neck.

Mark said, "Hey. Quit. Stop."

Bill let his head go and pushed him hard enough to almost knock him down.

Mark caught his balance, squared up to Bill. "I . . . man . . . *Don't.*" He was almost crying.

Smiling, Bill said, "Wait until you're a man, tough guy. Wait until the bar lights and the night's filled with skirts."

We went into the house, which was dark and even hotter than outside, like the inside of someone's mouth. Bill went to get his wallet. Mark went to put on a shirt. I waited in their front room, which would have been the living room for other renters, but for them it was a place for Pepsi cans and Wild Turkey bottles, a place to put boxes and sweat-stiff laundry, a place to plug in the beige rotary telephone with the cracked receiver and set it on the stained blue carpet in the corner. The T-shirt the woman had been wearing was folded neatly over the back of the only chair, a dark blue recliner with a torn armrest. I stared at it. I leaned over and smelled it. I smell it now.

Superfreak

We walked along the sidewalk in front of the new apartments. It was dusk. The sun shot tentacles of red light through the narrow alleys and building openings. These sidewalks had been hard for only a week or two, were still dark and wet-looking. A city trash truck roared slowly past us, its garbage-eating rear chewing on bags.

"People don't lock their doors here," Mark said as the truck's noise subsided. "They think new means safe." He threw a rock. It clacked off some vinyl siding meant to look like grainy wood. "What idiots! One day I'm just going to walk through all these apartments putting shit in my pockets." He scuttled ahead of me, theatrically, as if his pants were suddenly heavy, buckling his knees. "I'm stuffed with money! My ass is a coin dispenser!" He leaned over and shot a few imaginary coins—*ping, ping, ping*—out of his asshole, which I dodged by lunging sideways, landing in the grass-seeded dirt. We laughed.

The apartment buildings had gone from having small, plush, green lawns in front of them and shutters on the facades and cars in the driveways to having sparse grass and stickers on the windows (MARKETT ALL-WEATHER WINDOW CORP.) and no doorknobs. A hundred feet farther along there were tire-rutted yards and glassless windows and wide-open doorways—torn, plastic construction sheeting flapping here and there in the light wind. Once we got close to the end of the row of apartments—maybe five minutes of walking—the last few buildings were wood shells, half-formed, giving off the sharp scent of sawdust and the dusty clay smell of concrete drying.

"Over here!" Rick James called to us.

Mark and I walked through one of the buildings, which only had walls in the front, giving the place the feel of a set for a Hollywood Western. I thought of *Gun Smoke*, my father's favorite television show, which we sometimes watched reruns of together; though not very often, now that I thought about it, because I'd grown, lately—filled with secrets as I was, afraid sometimes of my own thoughts—to feel uncomfortable in my father's presence, as if we were two magnets with opposite charges. Still, as I walked into the shell of the building, I imagined a couple of showgirls in red, low-cut dresses throwing ankle-booted high kicks, their blonde locks rounded up on top of their heads like glowing manes.

"I got the beast," Rick James said. The beast was what we called Milwaukee's Best, the cheapest beer available. "I saved you tikes some bones."

Rick James was a bearded guy in his late twenties, maybe early thirties, who worked as a laborer for various construction crews around town. His real name was Richard something. He lived with his elderly mother, whom I sometimes saw sitting in a bathrobe on her porch—smoke-colored hair, face looking boneless. He was always telling—making up—stories of his sexual exploits, so some older kids had started calling him "superfreak," which morphed into Rick James.

Rick drank like someone trying to kill himself. It was like watching a science experiment—his mouth a palsied spit dispenser, his head too heavy for his neck. He touched people, wept openly in public, his arms two things meant to topple nearby objects, which suddenly seemed to *get in the way*. I had once found him sleeping in the woods. I thought he was dead, took off for home, keeping quiet, not wanting to be the kid in the paper who found the body.

Later I was surprised to see him, walking along the highway, hitchhiking—pasty, dirt-stained, bits of his hair on end as if he had just gotten out of bed. On Tuesday mornings he was usually sober, though, drinking coffee at the 7-Eleven, on his way to a construction site, the past several days lost, as if carved right out of his thoughts. Thursdays after work, broke, shaking, he'd buy beer for kids as long as the kids—Mark and I tonight—paid for and shared the booze.

I sat down a few feet from Rick on the exposed cinder-block foundation in the back of the building. Mark sat on the plywood floor. Someone had taken bright orange spray paint, the kind used to mark gas and sewer lines before backhoes go digging, and written SUCK MY MOTHERS DICK and PARTY TIL U DIE on some plywood leaning against the two-by-four studs.

Rick passed us each a beer from the twelve-pack. He was wearing blue work pants, a filthy white V-neck T-shirt with greenish-brown oval stains under the arms, and scuffed brown boots with short, white, broken shoestrings holding them tight.

"Thanks," Mark said, popping the beer open.

Rick chugged the first beer and crushed the can. He was sturdier with some alcohol, the first sips of which seemed to have magical healing properties. He was more than twice our size—maybe 210 pounds to our 100 and 105.

I drank as fast as I could, trying to get buzzed, belching between gulps.

"Why don't you guys take your shirts off? Man, it's hot," Rick said.

"I'm not hot," Mark said.

"Me neither," I said.

"It's pretty hot. You'd be more comfortable if you took off your shirts."

"I'm not taking mine off, Rick," Mark said.

Rick often asked us to take off some of our clothes, and there was a rumor that he and another guy who wandered around our city with headphones on liked to "doggy" each other, as we called it, out in the woods, but I don't know if that was true.

"Ashamed of your muscles?" Rick said.

"Not quite," Mark said.

Once it was clear we weren't going to take our shirts off, Rick chugged another beer and threw the crushed can against a stack of boards. "That young Jim Creedy is a prick," he said. He was into his third beer. He seemed drunk already. He started raging along in his story, only half making sense. "His daddy gave him that business and he thinks he's king of something," he went on. "Thinks he's better than everyone. Can't even drive a fucking nail straight. Sits in his truck drinking coffee half the fucking day with a CB in his hand."

59

"Yeah, I know that guy," Mark said. "Football player in high school. Had a hot girlfriend, too. She got into college and dumped his ass."

"Right," Rick said. "That's him. That's Creedy junior. Prick fired me today. Said I was sleeping in the bathroom I was supposed to be caulking. I was *resting my eyes* after about six hours of work is what I was doing. He's never heard of a break?"

"Too bad," I said. "But construction crews are all over the place, man. Don't worry about it." I wanted him to shut up and pass me a second beer before he drank them all.

"But he knows *everyone*," Mark said. "He could keep you out of work."

"You think?" Rick said.

"Oh, yeah, man," Mark said. "My dad talks about the Creedys all the time. They're like the construction mafia. If they bid a job, they get it. If they fire you, you're toast."

"Great," said Rick. "*Won*derful. Now what am I going to do?"

I looked at Mark. He smiled, that troublemaking smile, when Rick was looking down at his fourth beer—sulking, you could say. We heard the trash truck again, groaning beside a construction dumpster out in front of the building.

"Hey," Mark said to Rick. "I have an idea. I know what you can do."

Rick looked up from the beer. "What?"

Mark pointed to the noise of the truck. He had a buzz already—you could tell by the watery eyes, the smiling. "You could work"—he was laughing now, could barely finish his sentence—"on the trash truck."

Then he nearly doubled over, cracking up.

Rick smiled, slowly, watching him.

I took that as a cue and smiled, though it wasn't really funny.

The temperature had dropped, and the sunlight was disappearing, and everything was gray-blue with evening and shadow.

The full beer can missed Mark's head by inches. It crashed off a two-by-four wall stud and then landed on the floor, spinning and spewing foam.

Then motion, the stomp of boots, yelling: "Hey hey hey hey."

I was already up and moving. I jumped onto the cinderblock foundation, like a character in a barroom brawl in my father's favorite TV show.

I turned toward the shouting. In the blueness I could make out Mark on his hands and knees, but the sound, his sound, was echoing, and it seemed to be coming from the gutless building itself, a commotion elsewhere, as if from rowdy saloon customers, or from the future tenants, with all their problems, throwing their voices around in the half-built floors above us.

One of Rick's brown boots with sneaker strings ground down on the fingers of Mark's left hand. Mark was pinned to the floor, struggling to get free. Rick leaned over and pulled Mark's shirt violently over his head so that I could see the shadows of his rib cage like thin zebra stripes. Mark tried to pull away, but Rick took aim at the top of the captured arm, below the shoulder, and landed punch after hard punch— maybe ten, maybe fifteen—which sounded like a tenderizer pounding out a piece of meat.

Years later Rick got busted in the back of a high school kid's car with an ounce of wet, stinky psilocybin mushrooms. And years after that, when I was in college, I heard about him getting warned for spying on a mourning widow every Sunday afternoon at her husband's grave, in a quiet cemetery set back among trees. And still years after that, when I was a grown man and far from that place, I heard a rumor that he'd been found in possession of a barely working, unregistered handgun; though what kind of gunslinging he had in mind I couldn't guess. It didn't occur to me at twelve, already a drinker and drug taker, that I might end up like Rick James, desperate and lonely and dangerous. And it didn't occur to Mark, of course, that he *would* end up like Rick James in his way: a forward-moving disaster, leaving bounced checks and subpoenas and injury in his wake.

A week after the incident in the half-built apartments, on a Thursday evening, Mark's hand still rose-colored and swollen, still faintly boot-imprinted, his arm still stiff from the beating, we saw Rick in front of the 7-Eleven, sweaty and fidgety and forcing a smile. "Hey," he said, walking toward us, palms up, hands shaking, his face halfway between a cringe and a smile. "Hey. Don't walk away. Hey. *Listen.*"

7

Mothers

"You're not holding it in long enough," Mark said. We had just crawled through an open window into his mother's rental house, a sun-bleached colonial with moss clinging to the foundation, greening the cracks between the brick steps. We were in his mom's girlfriend's stepson's stepbrother's bedroom.

Mark had threatened his mom a few days before, said—not seriously, but said nonetheless—that he wanted her dead, was going to save his allowance to hire a hit man. He didn't know how to hire a hit man, obviously. But his mom had stopped taking his late-night phone calls. She had also made Bill take back Mark's key to her house. So Mark had said, "She doesn't want me there? Screw her. Let's break in."

"I'm trying," I said now, holding the woodshop-carved pot pipe, sitting on the stepson's stepbrother's skateboard, moving it back and forth on the thick, dull-green carpet, my back against the fake wood paneling of the room.

Mark grabbed the pipe, disappointed in me, and lit it with a yellow Bic, circling the flame around the edges of the foil covering the bowl as he sucked the end. It was ditch weed, dry and harsh, like inhaling near a campfire. His cheeks inflated; his eyes reddened. Seeds sparked and popped.

I coughed. My throat felt scraped. I shut my eyes tight, and little blue flecks went spinning in the deep darkness of my eyelids.

A few minutes later, I noticed my tongue, the size and shape of it. It was drying out and inflating, becoming a salted slug.

Mark was giddy, distant. "*Dude*," he laughed.

I laughed, too, couldn't stop myself, mostly at the laughing itself, which was all over the place, like something spilled.

The house hummed. Houses were machines, with wires and switches. I couldn't stop laughing.

A dull ache bloomed behind my eyes.

I thought, for a very long time I thought, of when Gerry H. put his thumb on my eyelid when I was eight and said, "I could pop it and probably kill you." I thought, for a very long time I thought, of how some bigger kids in the neighborhood who did not hate me but did hate Gerry H. held him by his wrists and ankles, facing down, so that his bare stomach was just inches from a new pile of dog shit, how the whole episode was like a masterfully devised torture system in which the tortured had to keep wriggling with an increasingly tired back and arms and legs to avoid having fresh, smelly feces spread across his belly, how when the fresh smelly feces was finally smeared across the tortured one's body it was not, of course, the fault of the torturers but simply a failure of fortitude and rightness on the part of the one being tortured.

My heartbeat was jumpy. I waited, trying to make it slow down. I tried to remember what I was waiting for a minute later, why I was concentrating on something having to do with my body. I worked hard to remember my lost thought until finally I remembered that maybe I hadn't lost a thought but was instead getting stuck in the feeling, the sort of mentally sick feeling, of a thought lost and needing to be tracked down again. This was something that sometimes happened to me when I took drugs: a feeling of increasing negativity and dislocation from self that seemed to slowly expand until I was near panic.

I looked around: dirty socks and T-shirts and jeans on the floor; on the walls were posters of Judas Priest, Black

Sabbath, the glistening bodies of women in bikinis, one with beer foam dripping, thick and white, down her large, shining chest. She was looking down, looking at me, smiling. She wouldn't leave me alone. She kept looking, kept staring. Who could talk to a woman like that? My face would lock, my jaw would rust tight, my bloated tongue wouldn't have an inch of wiggle room inside my mouth and I'd choke. *Please*, lady. I looked at a Budweiser ad—horses, huge hairy-footed Clydesdales—on the back of the fist-imprinted door. Over there: Stroh's. And Old Milwaukee. I lingered over a chipped, flesh-colored ashtray on the green bedspread in the shape of a pleading, open hand. I felt the way my mouth tasted—*radiated*, I wanted to say. *Irradiated. Earradiated. Hereradiated. Hairradiated.*

Mark put on a record. He was still here. Who knew? We listened to one of the stepson's stepbrother's albums. It was satanic, suicidal—and I just kept growing away from myself.

I closed my eyes. Just for a second. I opened my eyes. The music had stopped.

Empty room. Mark was gone.

The door was open. I stood up and walked out of the room. "Mark," I said, but not loudly, afraid now that we weren't alone. In a whispered half-hiss: "*Mark.*"

I walked slowly down a brown-carpeted hallway with

more fake wood-paneled walls. On these walls were pictures of families at Christmas, elderly couples leaning their heads toward each other and smiling, babies sitting amid blocks and rattles, happy, in that captured instant, to be having their picture taken. It occurred to me that one of these babies was probably Mark. I couldn't guess which one, though. They just looked like babies, round and rosy and bald. Little humans. Weird creatures locked up in frames. I had a thought about babies and God, but it escaped through my eyes. The last picture frame in the hallway was crooked and empty, the particle board backing visible.

I went out into a main room, where a card table was set up, papers stacked neatly on top of it. A TV rested on a metal rolling table covered in a rash of rust. A couple of lamps. Boxes around the table. The girlfriend must have been an accountant, or a bookkeeper. Mark's mom—I think I remember—was a nurse in a kid's ward.

My lips stuck together. I unsealed them. "Mark," I said again, still not very loudly, heading into a dark den with red carpet and missing light-switch covers and shafts of slanting sunlight cutting diagonally through. The room was filled with more boxes of papers—phone records, bills, receipts, tax forms, the recorded history of perhaps hundreds and hundreds of people. Facts, facts, facts and no sense to be found. I felt my insignificance like a breeze. I walked slowly around the room, looking in the boxes, then out the window into the bright day, at a dog in a neighbor's yard panting, a rusting grill inside of an oil-stained carport across the street, an old pickup parked along the curb of the house.

At the other side of the room, I could see through an open door, into a blue-tiled bathroom. The translucent shower curtain was half-open, exposing the faucet and showerhead, soap scum and shampoo bottles, a little window high in the wall, black mold on the metal frame. I stopped at the doorway, thinking of the movie *The Shining*, which I had just seen for the first time, the scene where the beautiful naked woman turns into an old woman with rotting skin and the soundtrack rises up into a synthetic and shrill crescendo of horror, and I was able to see now that Mark had gone through the medicine cabinet, leaving the mirrored door half open, and I felt my stomach, just then, seize and a faintness pass over me like the shadow of an airplane.

The house smelled of mildew and bodies and cardboard and soap and recently cooked food. It contained information about people—records, receipts, evidence. I recognized everything—it was my world, I knew that—but it looked and smelled foreign, unknown. I was walking through the edge of Mark's daydream, through senselessness, through a feeling I wanted to called *sickness*.

I thought *I have to get out of here* hard enough that it

escaped my mouth as words. I saw myself handcuffed, being put into the back of a squad car, ducking my head as people took pictures of me in my moment of shame: KID ROBBER CAUGHT! WHAT'S HAPPENED TO AMERICAN KIDS? I saw my mother and father as they signed papers about me at the station. I saw my father's teeth-clenched face, his anger face, saw him hitting me with his belt as he held me by the back of the shirt and I ran useless circles inside my small bedroom.

I headed through the kitchen, toward a door that went out into the backyard, where I could jump a fence and disappear into the woods.

I caught something at the periphery of my vision. On the refrigerator were several magnets holding up notes. I walked nearer. One magnet, I noticed, was holding up a crimped and crinkled picture of an eight- or nine-year-old Mark wearing a baseball uniform, posing as if about to field a grounder. I stared for a moment before I started to understand what I was looking at—the picture from the hallway's empty frame. In small black, block letters across the figure of the young Mark it said:

I LOVE YOU BUT YOU DON'T LOVE ME
YOU LOVE ME BUT I DON'T LOVE YOU
I LOVE ME BUT YOU LOVE YOU
YOU LOVE YOU BUT I LOVE ME

Staring at the note in that empty kitchen, in that humming house, I heard, or thought I heard, a car out on the street, a door slam, the faint sound of voices.

I moved quickly, heart sprinting, out the back door, through the backyard, ducking under a low-slung clothesline.

I jumped a fence out behind an old, leaning shed, landing on the edge of a wooded lot, running and running and running through trees and brush, stepping over beer and soda cans, scraps of paper, until I came to a sidewalk along a far-off main road, where I put my hands in my pockets, walked coolly as the warm traffic fanned past, smelling of rubber and asphalt and gas.

Hours later I woke up in a flimsy lawn chair in the far corner of my vacationing neighbors' backyard—queasy, tired, with a brain-blanking headache.

I daydreamed, from my rickety seat, about walking inside my house. My mom was cooking, her back to me so that I couldn't see her face as I entered the room. Looking out the window, looking at her own reflection, speaking to it as if speaking to me, she said: "What have you been up to, Sugar?"

"Nothing," I said, which is what I always said, but today I needed this lie, and I would need this lie from then on, for the rest of my life, because I understood, or thought I understood, that if a mother had any idea of what her son's life was like, what his thoughts were like, what *he* was like, he might kill her by breaking her heart. With my eyes open I dreamed that there was a way to murder someone you loved and still leave a body intact to move about in the world, to take pictures and pay bills and take pills and park a car along a weather-spotted curb at the end of a day of work. It happened all the time, every day, in houses up and down these blocks.

Love

"That's what you do if you love someone, David," Mark said.

A Monday morning. Bird sounds, traffic noise. Power lines, carrying a million voices, slung over our heads. Sun midway up the eastern sky.

Mark and I had been walking around, kicking cans, throwing rocks at mailboxes, looking in house windows and at the faces of people driving by in cars, and now we were sitting on the curb in front of the 7-Eleven: cigarette butts, oil stains in the shape of Midwestern states, shoe-printed chewing gum, the shimmering heat of car engines, wafts of cool air coming out of the double glass doors behind us each time they opened.

David balanced beside us on his red beach-cruiser bike, the kind with big wheels and fenders and longhorn handlebars. He had one foot on the concrete, one on a pedal. He held a Slurpee cup, his blue tongue resting on his bottom lip.

"I mean, if you *love* someone," Mark continued. "Not just *like*. Only if you're *in love*. That's when you use this technique."

"Noooooooo," David said. He was tall for his age, with short, wavy blond hair. He wore high-water jeans, three-button shirts fastened to the top, and a blue Izod windbreaker even when it was in the nineties, like today. At fourteen he possessed the intelligence level of maybe a six-year-old. He looked like the televised version of a retarded kid, so who could doubt—what kid would even think to doubt?—the realism and authenticity of television.

"Oh," Mark said. "I thought you were in love. Never mind then."

"I *am* in love!" David shouted.

A woman in cutoff jeans, a tank top, and flip-flops turned and looked at David as she walked into the store, a cigarette hanging from her mouth.

"Then *do it*," Mark said.

I squinted in the brightness, my T-shirt rolled up in my hand, wet with sweat.

"Hey," Mark said, looking at me, shoulders shrugged, palms up. "When you're in love . . . ?"

We were talking about David's crush on Marie, a girl who wouldn't even speak to Mark or me. She was kind to David, though—a pity thing, the way certain girls love helpless animals, hang posters of big-eyed baby seals on their bedroom walls. The whole imagined romance was a big joke among us middle-school flunkies. We tormented David because he was stupid and weak. We shouted at and mocked Marie's beautiful body, her beautiful hair, her beautiful face, which made her walk with her back stiff, her eyes straight ahead. We had all felt an arm-twist to the point at which the bone creaked, had all tasted rusty blood in our mouths after a hard punch to the face, had all received wedgies from bigger kids that ripped open our ass cracks, had all had our ears boxed to ringing by our dads, uncles, brothers, coaches . . . It killed us that Marie wouldn't explode into tears for our amusement. It was the least she could do, with all that beauty and success, with the way she *knew* she was better than us.

"Dude," Mark said again. "Tell David. Tell him what to do."

I tried to avoid David, but we had played together some as small boys—at our mothers' insistence—and he always found me now, sidled over: "Hey!" Kids in my new clique, the tough kids, the cool kids, walked up and said, "Hey,

GREG BOTTOMS

David," and instead of patting him on the back they hit
him, sometimes hard—a gut shot, a pointy knuckle to the
arm, a smack to the face. He was shocked, hurt, but when
we laughed, he rounded the corner of his pain somehow and
laughed, too. Like me, he wanted to belong no matter the
obstacles. He was willing to be tortured, to an extent, if he
could be a part of the something I called kid life in our city.
I was willing to torture, to an extent, to not be left out of
that same something, which would have been like becoming a leper, or being banished into the wilderness to perish
among the stacked layers and layers of corpses of unwanted
and unliked kids.

"*Tell* him, dude," Mark said. "*Tell* him."

A guy named Darryl, a sixteen-year-old who'd spent time
in reform school, a kid who said "fuck" two or three times a
sentence, his language like an American poetic assault in its
way, textured and stylish and syntactically interesting, had
put a cigarette out on David's back not long before. I saw it
happen but didn't say or do anything. I'm sure I laughed like
all the other kids there.

I looked at the ground, at a cigarette butt with a circle of
lipstick around the filter, and thought about David screaming when Darryl burned him, his animal grunting, how he
pushed his elbows out behind him, his back curled away from
the pain, his bony scapula like little spread butterfly wings.

I looked up. "David," I said as I sat on the 7-Eleven curb, unrolling my shirt, sweating, my eyes like gun sights pointed right at his stupid face, "here is what I'd do . . ."

A few days from then, at school, on the playground, he would show his shriveled, asexual prick to Marie. She'd run away, *finally* crying. He'd then stand, bewildered, pants open, blank-faced, all hope, his whole world, ended; he'd drop to the ground and rub dirt into his hair and face, like a beast trying to cover its own bad scent. I once, years ago, said a long prayer about this. And I still have dreams about it. But in the dreams I'm the one with dirt on my hands, on my face, in my hair. I'm the idiot with my pants down.

Term-Paper Topics

"What do you know about war?" Mark said.

"I know all about war," Bill said. He was sitting on the old green couch, in a pair of white underwear and tube socks, eating from a Styrofoam carton of Chinese food. Whenever he was going to the Chinese place for takeout, he'd say, "Let's do chink tonight" or "Let's eat dog, fellas, let's us digest somebody's poor Fido."

Rusty, standing shirtless in a pair of jeans in the doorway between the den and kitchen, drinking a can of Pepsi, slowly and absent-mindedly massaging his crotch, said, "Hey, have you seen chink porn? That stuff is nasty. Slants'll do anything, hoss. Those foreigners are crazy.

Where do they get their ideas, know what I mean? They have this thing, hoss—I forget what it's called—where they get the"—he looked at Mark and me, back at Bill—"the man stuff, right, into a cup and drink it. Then they'll get a couple of hot me-love-you-longtimes to kissing and swapping it back and forth in their mouths while somebody's snapping pictures." He squinted his eyes, turned his mouth downward, as if disgusted.

There was a new flood of Vietnamese, Laotian, and Cambodian refugees in our area, so a lot of grown-ups seemed to be talking about "Asians." They worked down at the fish- and crab-processing plants (where I would later work as a teen) for an unlivable wage that allowed the plant owners—well-to-do white men—to make a slightly bigger profit than if they hired poor blacks from the surrounding neighborhoods. If you drove by the plants, down along the James River in the industrialized east end of Newport News, into that foul fish smell, you'd see twenty or thirty Asian refugees, all wearing white rubber boots, standing around outside, even in the rain and wind. They waited to get into the plants and start working. The people I knew had an ongoing complaint about work, lived for the weekend. Many songs on the radio commemorated this. Work, as I understood it then, was a specter, a running joke, or a thing romanticized into valorous myth, and it didn't make sense to me yet how it became one or another of these in the mind of the man telling the work story.

"I seen that," Bill was saying. "It does have a name. I think they got magazines about it." He looked at Mark and said, "Rusty was in the army."

"Yeah, I was in the Army when I was twenty for about six months," Rusty said. "I was getting into trouble and my old man talked me into signing up. My dad was a patriot, hoss, could skin a deer with an old screwdriver. We had an American flag big as a bed sheet flapping off the house when I was a kid. Sometimes I think the old bastard was hoping I'd catch a bullet or some shrapnel. But I was never sent over there. I was stationed in Mississippi. I got some pretty nice tang in Mississippi, but I got me some of them warts, too, like little cauliflowers hanging off my pecker. I've passed them suckers around alright. Lot of women are wondering who snuck a toad up there while they were sleeping." He laughed. "And I broke my hand on a black dude's face and tore some ligaments and shit all down my wrist and they shipped my ass home. I don't see a cent from the Army. Worst thing about the Army was the racial stuff. Just about had some wars in those barracks down there. Had white versus black football games and that was some hard hitting, hoss. They made the guy I punched a sergeant, which is messed up in all kinds of ways because a lot of Mississippi rednecks just weren't going to listen to someone like that. Hell, some of the white dudes refused to swim in the camp pool once the blacks got in the water. I wasn't like that. I don't just hate someone for being black. I mean, I wouldn't drink after a black person but there's chlorine in a pool. Ain't no way to win a war, though, having everybody pissed off and suspicious. But man, I was twenty. I was crazy and drunk and trying to get laid. I had me a short fuse, hoss. *Real* short. My daddy liked to have killed me. I've mellowed. I've grown up."

"You're an old man," Bill said, spooning greasy brown rice into his mouth. "An old man. But you'd have torn up some ass in 'Nam, wouldn't you have!"

"Lord, hoss, I'd have come back bloody and *limping* from all the killing I'd have done over there. I'd have shed my foreskin like a swollen snake in that jungle!"

After swallowing a mouthful of food, Bill said, "You'd've caught some stuff there, man. I've heard stories."

"Hoss," Rusty said, "I'd have just lopped it off and left it overseas for the rats when it was over."

They both laughed. I didn't know exactly what they were talking about. Killing? Lopping something off? I laughed. They looked at me.

Mark and I had to write an end-of-the-year seventh-grade term paper about the possibility of complete nuclear annihilation in a war with the Russians. This depressed me. I didn't like reading. The school had put me in an advanced English class the year before, in sixth grade, and I purposefully failed a couple of tests to get demoted back to the normal class, if not the remedial one, because my friends mocked me for being in a class with mostly girls. I avoided writing. Education was a bad job I had to get through each weekday from September to June. My grandfathers had dropped out of school; my grandmothers had dropped out. My father had dropped out of high school but then went back and finished at twenty; my older brother would do the same, a few years before homelessness and then prison; my younger brother and I would squeak by. My one hope for this term paper, I figured, was to write something based on the TV movie *The Day After*, which had just been on ABC. I'd write a paper about Steve Gutenberg, Jason Robards, and John Lithgow, about polluted drinking water in Lawrence, Kansas, where the story took place. Mark, on the other hand, had no idea how to proceed.

"I'm not going to do it," he said. "I don't care if I fail. I'll fail anyway."

Rusty sat down. Bill put his food down and stood up, as if preparing himself for something physical. I looked at him; it was like a pool ball was resting in the front of his briefs. No wonder women liked him. (I believed that all women really wanted was a gigantic prick, a "horse cock," as Rusty put it.) I wondered if that made me gay, looking at Bill, being so interested, so entranced, by his body all the time. I hoped not. The two gay kids I knew, the kids people *assumed* were gay because of their habits and effeminate affect, were picked on and punched, bullied and pushed around. If I were gay the best thing I could do to keep from being discovered, I figured, was to find one of these gay kids and punch him with someone around to see it.

"I'll help you," Bill said.

"You will?" Mark said. He had his dirty feet up on the coffee table. He had been looking at the ceiling. Now he looked at Bill.

"Yeah," Bill said. He threw his food carton across the room and it landed in the trashcan. "We'll get it done. How long does it have to be?"

"Four pages."

"Jesus! What are you, in college or something?"

"Seventh grade."

"Seventh grade? Huh, I just told a fella down at the lumber yard you was in sixth grade."

"Seventh."

"Damn, you're getting up there, aren't you?"

Rusty, crushing his Pepsi can, added, "Yeah, you got to write that paper, hoss. Do what they tell you to do. Follow their rules. It'll pay off. Play the game, hoss. Play the game."

"Right," Bill said. "You can fight them all you want, but it'll catch up to you. Better to just learn the rules and do what they say."

"Pay for it if you don't, that's for sure," Rusty agreed. "When my back hurts, I think, Should have stayed in school. When I'm putting powder on my rotten feet, I think, Should have stayed in school."

Who are "they," I wanted to ask. I backed away as Mark and Rusty and Bill talked about, strangely, the importance of getting our seventh-grade term papers turned in so "they" wouldn't penalize us, if not ruin or destroy us.

The conversation swelled toward something triumphant. Everyone got excited. Rusty suggested that Mark write about how not nuking Vietnam out of existence was a big mistake, how we should learn from that mistake and kill as many Russians as possible, just take out the whole country. Our term papers somehow became a story about the importance of working, but also about the deep unfairness of working, the lopsided playing fields of class and privilege, the ones we'd need to navigate if we ever wanted anything more than what our parents had.

I walked home to do my own term paper, to introduce Steve Gutenberg, Jason Robards, and John Lithgow, great political thinkers in a time of national stress. *These were men*, I imagined writing toward the end of my paper, *American history will not soon forget.* As I walked along the white line of the highway, kicking rocks and bottle caps and cigarette butts once again, stepping out of the way of truck mirrors whizzing by, I tried to imagine some face for the power that made all the adults I knew work and suffer.

Accidents

"It was raining that night," Hazel said. "Really pouring. There were no lights along the road."

Late morning. A Saturday. I was lying on Hazel's bed, on her pink-flowered bedspread with the handsome men from her posters staring down at us. Jealous of me, I imagined. Hazel lay on her back, looking up at the ceiling, sunlight thrown over her, window-slat shadows stretched across her stomach. I imagined us from above, as if we were in a movie—a movie in which we were about to have hot, carefully lit, and musically accompanied sex—and I wasn't almost a foot shorter than she was and my muscles were bigger and I didn't have braces or a first peppering of zits across my freckled chin, which would soon flare into an acne mask, and I was strong and sensible, the silent type with a hint of danger; I was a loner—no family problems, no family; men feared my strength; women wanted me, watched me as I walked down the street with the rustle of worn money, my arms bowed out because I was doing push-ups and pull-ups now. I had spent most of my morning looking into the bathroom mirror at the eight long, black hairs now sprouting from my armpits. I also had five wiry hairs above my penis, which I had thought of naming, but that would have been a stupid kid thing to do, so I didn't (though I did have names picked out in case I wanted to later).

I propped myself up on one elbow to better watch Hazel's lips move, her beautiful mouth and tongue and teeth move, to listen. She wouldn't let me touch her until she finished telling her stories. Sometimes it was just her hands and arms that I could touch; other times, her legs, the backs of her thighs; once her breasts, but only once, and briefly; often the small of her back, which she liked best. But first I had to hear a story. Each time, each touch, came with a story.

"They had had a big fight," she went on, talking to the ceiling. "These fights, they were unbelievable sometimes. Like murder, you know. People crashing around, breaking stuff. I mean, it just made the whole house *dark*. Sissy was just a kid, a baby really, and she would start crying, weeping, you know, and I'd hold her and try to be brave." She looked at me.

My gaze had drifted down her long body—the bulge of her breasts, the shadows across her stomach, the curve of her hip bones through her jean shorts, the light and shade and shine of her thighs. Now I looked at her face. I said, "Uh huh. Yeah."

"So she storms out of the house, gets into her car, you know, and starts driving." She paused. "OK. Wait a sec. Hold on a sec." She took a deep breath, let it go. Took another one, let it go. "So she *storms* out of the house, gets into her car, which my dad *bought* for her, and starts driving, driving like a madwoman, like a crazy woman, like a totally controlling loooonatic. And it all turns on her, in her brain, you know. She begins to regret everything. How she treated us. How she treated my father. Tears blur her vision. The pain is so, you know, *unbearable* and shit. Somehow she loses control of the car—the cops couldn't say how—and veers across the yellow line, tries to get control, and smashes into a tree. She *flies*"—she sat up abruptly—"through the windshield and out into a field, her whole face ripped and hideous and covered with *hot, dripping* blood."

Some bees kamikazied the window, pinging off the screen.

"You and these stories," I said. "One day you're going to be a horror writer. You'll make thousands."

"I think I'm going to be an actress, but I'll write on the side maybe, write my own movies," she said. "I mean, so many people think I'm definitely pretty enough, and I could take drama next year, maybe get into a play."

I smiled, hoping now that it was time to touch.

"Did you believe me?" she asked, lying back down on the bed.

"Believe you?" I said.

"I mean if you didn't know that I spent weekends with my mom, would you have believed that's what happened to her?"

"Of course," I said, willing to say anything in these moments.

"I bet if you remember me when you're older," she said, "I mean years and years from now, you'll have a memory of a tragic beauty, a girl who was very wounded and very strong, whose mother died in a horrible car accident." She leaned over and kissed me.

I said, "That's how I remember it already."

Hunters

We were smoking pot, Mark and I, some of his dad's new pot, and sitting on the porch of the old house, staring down at the dirt below through a three- or four-foot hole where a section of floorboards had rotted away and broken, giving it the look of an open mouth full of busted, jagged teeth.

This abandoned farmhouse was out in the woods, on the outskirts of our city. It was an old, leaning structure, once white, now speckled gray; all the windows had been kicked out, and bits of triangular glass lay around the foundation, refracting light. Inside, graffiti covered the walls. Outside, out here on the porch, you could hear traffic on the main road a half-mile away.

We had walked here past the new apartments and the new shopping mall (right next to the abandoned, old shopping mall), through neighborhoods, across baseball fields and empty parks, and today, like every day we came to the house to hang around, I had a fear-inducing sense of time. This had something to do with drugs and drinking at a young age, but it was beyond that, too, a feeling of stepping outside time and being able to view it as an unstoppable force, an implacable thing unconcerned with me or anyone else, something I wished I could capture and contain, the way that naked woman was contained in the Polaroids under Bill's bed, like an insect in amber. I wanted to feel, as all humans want to feel, that I was the gravitational center of meaning, but out here it somehow slipped away. This house was a place where people—a family—had once lived and then disappeared, with almost no trace of them left at all. The woods and moss and vines had grown up around the house, partly overtaken it, rotted it away, as if the earth was reclaiming a spot only temporarily inhabited by things it needed to get rid of.

I heard a rustle out in the trees.

"What are you fucking fags doing?" Darryl said.

We looked up. Darryl had shoulder-length, sandy-blond

hair, feathered. He was maybe five-foot-eight, a hundred and sixty pounds, thick with muscles. He wore jeans and a dark-blue T-shirt with the sleeves cut off, and beat-up sneakers. His shirt was ripped wide open, so you could see his ribs, the soft, low part of his sides. To Mark and me, Darryl was almost a demonic presence in our city—popping up unexpectedly to shower misery down upon us. The only person I feared more was my sixteen-year-old, black-belt brother, who was—though I did not know this at the time—in the unpredictable early throes of severe mental illness.

Mark said, "We're looking into this hole."

"Why the fuck are you stupid fucks looking into a stupid fucking hole?" Darryl said. "I think you two are fucking getting high and then you're going to fucking suck each other off out here where no one can fucking see you. That's what I fucking think." He clumped up the weathered, half-broken steps onto the porch, darkening it.

I couldn't say anything. I thought Mark might say something—he was the talker—but he didn't. I'd had a few tokes and once again strange meanings went floating out of people's face-holes like clouds of gnats. Darryl, I figured, was probably going to do something terrible (once he had smashed our skulls together and I ended up with "cauliflower" ear, an injury boxers and wrestlers get, my ear soft and blue-gray and ballooned up around the top like a grape).

"I fucking killed this fucking bird on the way here," Darryl said. He reached into his back pocket and dropped a small robin onto the splintered porch boards. "I hit it with a fucking rock and stunned it and then I fucking kicked it as hard as I fucking could." He laughed. "I kicked the fucking shit out of it, man."

Its skull, the size of a gumball from one of those bubble-gum machines at the front of grocery stores (over near the quarter-per-ride clown car), was crushed. One of the wings stretched out awkwardly to the side. A few tiny ants went busily about its back. I stared down into its black marble eye. It was dead all right, because I could see that it no longer had a soul, no glimmer of light at all.

"Give me that fucking joint, fag," Darryl said.

I quickly handed it to him.

He wiped the unlit end of the joint. "You fucking spit on it, you fucking fag." He looked right into my eyes. "I bet you two fucks," he said, taking a toke, his voice a little higher now, "come out here and fucking do a big-time fucking suck off. Yeah, I think that's exactly what you fucking do."

He sat down beside the bird, across from Mark and me, and smoked the whole joint without giving it back or saying anything more.

We could do nothing. I imagined myself as a powerful assassin breaking his neck with quick jujitsu. Then I imagined myself as a hit man in a black suit, blowing his brains out with a big black gun with a silencer the size of a large dildo (Rusty had just explained to Mark and me what a dildo was) while some cool blues guitar played in the background and the audience viewed me from a low camera angle, which made me *tower* impressively. We stared at the bird, the feathers matted with blood, the misshapen head. I started to wonder how many people had died in this house, figuring at least one but maybe as many as five or six. How many dead birds had been on this property? Pets? Rodents? Insects? I figured Darryl would eventually kill someone, and years later I heard he went after his dad with a tire iron or a crowbar, a sledgehammer maybe. Stories, stories, and more stories. Who can keep track? I assume he is in jail now.

Once the joint was just about gone, Darryl spit a stringy bit of saliva onto the roach and then ate it, which sent a lunch-taste—Doritos, Pepsi—up into my throat.

Within a minute of swallowing the joint, he started rubbing his face and quietly moaning. A transformation took place. When he moved his hands and blinked repeatedly, his eyes were the color of bricks and his face was pale with a bluish tint. I felt relieved. He seemed less dangerous. I saw us jamming him into a furnace. I imagined putting my foot on his throat and saying something scene-ending.

"What the fuck was in that fucking stuff, man?" he said. "Holy fucking shit."

"It was just pot," Mark said. "My dad's weed. It's pretty strong, though. He buys it from this black drywall guy named Leon. He's from Atlanta. So that was like Georgia mountain pot, man. I've never seen anyone smoke a whole big joint like that by themselves, not even Rusty or my dad. You even ate the roach. You're in new territory, dude. Get ready."

"Wow, man," Darryl said. "Wow. Why didn't you fucking *say* that? I'm fucking blasted. My hands are fucking tingling and my ears are ringing and the trees look all fucking blurry except for the one I'm fucking looking at. My fucking eyes. The trees are like trying to fucking hide from my fucking focus so I can't ever find them. The trees are fucking ducking behind the trees. I don't fucking feel like I'm fucking breathing right either, man. What did you guys fucking let me do, man?"

"OK, man," Mark said, standing up. "Be cool. Try to relax." He looked at me like: "Let's go."

"I fucking saw that," Darryl said.

"Saw what?" I said.

"Saw how he fucking looked at you. You gay bitch-ass fuckers are fucking fucking with my ass, man. You think I fucking killed this fucking bird on fucking purpose, don't you? You think I'm a fucking bird murderer and that's what the fucking tree hiding is fucking about. Man, why are you guys fucking doing this to me." He was almost whimpering. "I thought you were my fucking friends, man. How was I supposed to know I could hit that fucking bird?"

Friends?

"You shouldn't have smoked that much," Mark said. "You should have shared that. I mean, you're basically rewiring some of your brain."

"Don't," Darryl half-shouted, rubbing hard at his eyes, the whimpering now high-pitched and hoarse, "don't fucking say that shit to me, man. Fucking fuck." He lay down on the porch, turned onto his side, back onto his back, back onto his side. "I'm really fucking uncomfortable, man." He got into the fetal position. "I feel like there is some evil fucking shit going on inside me right now. I'm in that fucking movie *Alien*, man. I'm on the fucking *table*, man."

"We're going to go," Mark said.

"Yeah, we're going," I said, standing up.

"Don't go!" Darryl screamed, still in the fetal position. "You got to help me. Please help me." He was drooling onto the porch. "I didn't fucking mean to kill that bird, man. I know what you fucking guys are fucking thinking, man, and you're wrong about me. You're all fucking wrong about me. It was weird. I fucking thought about killing it and then it fucking died. My thoughts made it fucking happen."

He huffed and snotted. He went back to moving his legs

around and it was like he was dancing in slow motion, or swimming in shallow water.

He said, "Oh, God, man. Oh, God."

Then he sat up abruptly.

Mark and I stepped back, ready to run if he came at us.

He shook his head and rubbed his eyes again. He stood up slowly and took a few wobbly steps over to the dead bird. He knelt and leaned down over it, like someone about to pray.

"I'm going to fucking eat this fucking bird, man," he said. He was almost crying, which I wouldn't have imagined possible half an hour before.

We watched as he picked it up and walked down the steps, into the patchy grass and dirt. He was wobbly on his feet, but he handled the robin as if there were nothing more delicate. "I'm not going to fucking let this fucking bird die for fucking nothing. I'm going to fucking eat it like a fucking hunter. I'm a fucking hunter, man. I'm fucking going to fucking eat my fucking kill, man. It's the only fucking way. And you fucking guys have to be my fucking witnesses, OK, you like have to fucking watch me eat it all, OK, so that I can fucking . . . Jesus fucking Christ, man, what is with these *trees*?"

Mark and I gathered some sticks, dry pine needles, and brush. Darryl sat in the dirt, holding the bird as if it were alive. We made a circle of rocks and started a fire with Mark's Bic and a crushed paper cup out in what was once a front yard. After a minute, smoke went chugging up into the high pines and I thought someone from the neighborhood that was only about a quarter of a mile away would call the fire department any time now.

Once the fire was going, Darryl came out of his trance and with the bird still held gently in his hand he went and found a sharp stick. He came back and pushed it into the side of the bird, twisting it until it went through, which made a *pop* and then a suction kind of noise. He made us sit with him as he cooked it black over the open fire, the feathers smelling almost sweet as they burned away and fell into the flames.

It wasn't easy to eat the bird. Darryl had to use a sharp piece of window glass, which I went and got for him over by the house, to rip open the belly and scrape out some of the smoldering gut stuff, and we watched, astonished, absolutely enthralled, as he crunched into the body and had to spit out most of what he was trying to eat—bones, burned feathers, finally the beak, the eyes. He made a good show of it, but he didn't actually get much down, maybe a charred ounce of bird flesh.

Afterward, he stumbled around, not talking at all. He was delirious, and it was hard to tell if he was poisoned by the bird and weird plants and sticks we burned to cook it, or if he had just smoked so much strong pot that he finally needed to pass out, to be released from consciousness until his mind was better able to sync back up with the world, or probably it was a combination of all this.

He walked up onto the porch, right to where the little spot of blood from the bird was—"Look at this blood," he said—and threw up what looked like everything he had eaten in his life—a beige and black torrent. This, the whole theatrical episode—his spitting and gagging and bubbling—lasted longer than seemed natural or even maybe survivable. Then he stood up straight, his eyes rolled back to white like an attacking great white shark's, reeled backward, and then fell through the hole in the porch floorboards, into the house's mouth with the jagged teeth, hitting his head on the way down.

Mark and I scrambled up onto the porch, avoiding the giant puddle of puke, which smelled like shit and chemicals. We looked down into the hole and could see Darryl among the shadowy dampness three feet below.

"Man," Mark said, "he is *wasted*."

Silence from below.

"Is he dead?" I said. It was dark in the hole, hard to see.

"No," Mark said. "He's not dead because I can see his chest moving a little bit. He's breathing, I think. His breathing is off, but I doubt he'll die. It'd be pretty cool if he died, though. There'd be a lot of happy people."

I looked at the smoldering fire. I went and threw dirt on what was left of it. I tried to make sure there were no glowing embers because I knew a kid, an eighth-grader, who lit a piece of cardboard box just screwing around and it blew into some bushes near a house and the fire department came and that kid's dad—I can't remember the kid's name—beat him like a prisoner of war right out in their side yard with several neighbors watching, which had to be embarrassing.

Mark stayed on the porch, staring down at Darryl. "I hate this bastard, man," he said. "I should take a leak on him."

"He'll kill you when he wakes up if you do," I said. "He'll kill me, too. So don't do it. Don't get me killed, man."

Mark came down the steps. He picked up a small stick from the ground, turned around, and threw it up onto the porch, near the hole, the vomit. It clacked off the weather-scarred wall and bounced off the porch into the weeds. He then bent down and picked up a rock and threw it up toward the hole, but that missed, too. I threw a pine cone. I threw a stick. Mark threw a crushed, rusted can. We started throwing rocks, pine cones, trash, and sticks up toward the hole, mostly missing, but still laughing, enjoying our moment of power.

Eventually we walked back in the direction of the neighborhoods, toward nothing in particular. I imagined some kids a hundred years from now finding Darryl's bones among foundation rubble and tall, tall trees. I imagined a kid going into the basement of a space-aged building, to do laundry or something, and finding small pieces of Darryl's skull but never knowing what they were, maybe keeping them in a jar, the mystery only deepening as the centuries passed. Mark joked and laughed. I barely paid attention to him, thinking about how the day had turned out better than it could have.

In the Woods

"Whatever happened to Bulldog, anyway?" I asked.

"I think Rusty shot her," Mark said.

"Shot her?"

"Yeah," Mark said. "Bill said if Rusty took the dog and kept her in his apartment until someone bought her they could split the money."

"He shot her?"

"She was messing everything up, but she liked Rusty for some reason. Women, crazy people, dogs—everybody likes Rusty. It's weird. Guy's a dick. Anyway, then he got kicked out of the apartment because the dog bit the guy who owned the building and he needed to come live here, so Bill said to get rid of the dog." Mark smiled. "Rusty parked the Chevelle along the highway and walked Bulldog out into the woods and shot her in the head a couple of times with his little .22 pistol. He wrapped the gun in a dish towel so it wouldn't make so much noise. He buried Bulldog a couple hundred yards from the highway. Out by Dixie Digg's RV lot."

"How do you know all that? You just said you *thought* he killed her."

"Bill said in a roundabout way. And I've heard Rusty bragging about it. They're trying to keep it a secret. I don't think it's legal to shoot a dog. I'm pretty sure it's not."

"I thought Bill was going to get a bunch of money for the dog."

"At first, but then my mom said she should get half. So Bill was like, 'No way, witch, I'm not buying your dyke paints,' and told Rusty to get rid of the dog and he could stay here. So Rusty got rid of her. No one would buy that dog anyway, dude. Money down the drain."

"*Man,*" I said.

He was smiling.

Then I said, "You're lying, aren't you?"

"The dog went to the pound, dude," he laughed. "You should have seen your face! You should have seen your face! You should have seen your face!"

"You're an idiot," I said.

Still laughing, he aimed a finger pistol at his temple, dropping his cocked thumb, sending—one would have to imagine—his whole barking self right out the other side of his head.

13

A Situation

"Time to move on," Rusty said. He and Bill were sitting in old lawn chairs in the backyard, drinking beer. It was ten in the morning, a Sunday. "I think she's the one. She is. I know she is. I think so. I think she might be. Yep, she's the one."

Mark was inside getting his shoes on. I sat on the back porch, behind Rusty and Bill. Bill was going to pay Mark and me five bucks to split between us if we picked up all the sticks and branches in the yard, which were all over the place from a recent storm.

"Sounds good," said Bill. "You've always got a couch."

"Thanks," Rusty said. A minute later: "She's got a kid, though."

"Oh, boy. How old?" asked Bill.

"Nine, ten, something like that."

"Kid's ain't so bad," Bill said.

"But his dad still comes around," Rusty said. "Was kind of giving me the eye the other day. I liked to've smacked that look off his face."

"Sure. Sure. Perfectly normal," Bill said. "Y'all just have to adjust to each other, though. You got a situation. A situation. Everybody's got to feel out the situation."

"Right," said Rusty. "I know. But the kid's a little crappy bastard himself. Barely talks to anybody. Gets in a lot of trouble at school, too, I hear."

"You got to teach a kid," said Bill.

"I hear you," said Rusty.

"But feel it out, get used to the situation," said Bill, taking a drink. "Once you're a part of things then it becomes your responsibility to tell a kid and get him to do right. Especially if you're kind of the father figure in the house and no one else is teaching him."

"I hear you, hoss."

Mark came out back and we started picking up the sticks and putting them in a corroded wheelbarrow. Rusty and Bill both cracked open another beer.

It was hot, bright. Fat clouds kept just missing the sun. Mark and I worked hard, the men's eyes on us.

Bill stared at Mark, ready to criticize the way he worked if he slacked off. He took another drink.

After a while, Rusty said, "It's a shame women have to have babies like they do."

"A situation," Bill said. "It's a situation."

14

Break Up

"I want to break up," Hazel said. She had her head sticking out of her front door.

I was standing on the porch, under clouds and invisible stars and some kind of—I had to assume—narcoleptic God.

She said, "I'm getting back with Clark because Clark is sixteen and everybody likes him. He drives."

I looked at her, studied her face, which was, still is, my paradigm for beauty. My soul fell down through my body and got wrapped around my ankles like a pair of baggy jeans. I could have stepped right out of it and left it there and someone could have looked into my empty eyes, the way I did with Darryl's bird, and they wouldn't have seen any light, none at all. Our souls only plague us, I think sometimes—I certainly thought then—remind us of something we can't remember that nevertheless seems forever and painfully lost. "OK," I said. "Whatever," I said.

"Don't ever come back here," Hazel said. "Clark is cool. So I've decided to not like you anymore."

"Whatever," I said.

"Do you want me to say why I'm dumping you?" she said.

"No."

"I had this dream," she went on anyway. "There was a car parked in front of my house, but the lights were so bright and it was so dark out that I couldn't tell who it was. I didn't know why they were there. It was kind of scary. I was wearing my favorite dress and looking out my window. I walked downstairs, through a dark, empty house—somehow I knew I was alone—and then out the front door. I watched myself walk toward the lights, you know, and they were like the sun almost, or like stadium lights or something. I was frightened for myself. I mean I was frightened as I watched myself in the dream. When I turned the corner and got past the lights, it was Clark inside the car, behind the wheel. He didn't have a shirt on. He was smiling and handsome. I felt all this *love*, total love, you know. But when he tried to talk, no sound came out of his mouth. It was kind of weird. Kind of scary. He was trying to tell me something important. I was all sweaty when I woke up. That was a message, I think, so I need to be with him for now. Sorry."

I walked away, but, luckily, the dream stuff helped me out—it was my finest friend at twelve—and it rolled over me like a tide so that I forgot my loss and shame for a moment and became part of the summer day with its haze and stillness and drifted slowly past the insect-singing trees and the sulfur-smelling creek sizzling in the sun and the 7-Eleven and the strip mall and the car dealership (BIG JULY 4TH SALE—BUY AMERICAN) and into the woods and out of the woods and into the woods again, through the glassless front window of the apartment building being built in the next neighborhood over and out of the back opening where a sliding-glass door would one day be, landing in the churned-up, bulldozer-tracked dirt and stepping—*boom*—back into the flow of time.

Somehow, though, I was standing in Hazel's backyard, among her flowers. I thought I might lie down for a while, in her suicide spot.

She stuck her head out of her bedroom window. She said, "If you don't get out of my flowers I'm going to have to call my dad at work. We'll press charges."

My first love.

15

Fight

Mark came out of the back bedroom of his hot, dark house, shirtless, with eight or ten of the Polaroids of the naked blonde woman from the box under Bill's bed duct taped to his bare, bony chest and stomach. He had on his blue corduroy shorts, socks, and the construction boots he sometimes wore when he earned extra money helping Bill out by cleaning up at a job site. He was holding a half-drunk forty-ounce bottle of Milwaukee's Best.

It was the day of the fight. I was nervous, feeling absent from myself again, had spent the better part of the morning in the bathroom, stomach churning, talking tough in the mirror. I said, "What's with the pictures?"

He took a long pull from the bottle. "Protection," he said. "Maybe he won't want to punch this woman in the sweet spot. *Please, Darryl*"—his voice high—"*don't hurt my nice cooch.*" He smiled. Then he looked at his boots. "Steel toe. Teeth removers."

He had muscles like—like what?—like a gerbil, like a hamster. He barely showed any evidence of having entered puberty. Darryl, with his mustache and weight, was going to kill him.

"Don't go," I said. "It'll take him a while to get to you."

"I'm going, dude." He took a drink. "I'm feeling good." He belched. "Bill said, 'Never back down.' Bill said, 'Take a beating but don't ever run.'" He slow-moed a punch combo with the bottle in his hand, careful not to spill. "I'm going to fuck him up. Rusty said, 'First punch, first punch. Relaxed, just checking the situation, *wham*. And the face. And the face. And the face. And the throat.' Rusty said, 'Bite nuts, thumb eyes, bend fingers.'"

"You're going to die," I said.

"We're friends."

"Friends. I'll pull him off you."

"You can't help. If I put up a good fight, he'll leave me alone. 'Respect,' Rusty said, 'that's all a man needs.' Square up. Face. Throat. Eyes. Nuts. Nobody's going to take from me. Nobody's going to intimidate me. Nobody's going to crowd me out. I'm a man, *bitch*. I'm a man, *faggot*." More punches—*pah pah pah*.

It was the late morning; we were off, walking along that grid of city streets I can still see vividly even now—all these years, all these *lifetimes*, later—past the school and the basketball courts, the fields and neighborhoods, the strip mall and the car dealership and the diner. Mark did look pretty cool, pretty Mad Max, shirtless and half-drunk, with pictures of a naked woman taped all over his chest like so much armor. Some people beeped as they drove by. We raised our fists—shirtless warriors. Who was going to take down a couple of badass twelve-year-olds like us?

We went past Hazel and Sissy's house. Mark said, "Dumped you?"

I said, "Dumped her. She's crazy, man. Totally psycho. Wouldn't leave me alone. Crazy bitch."

"Over there enough."

I wanted to say, *I love her*. I wanted to tell him that I couldn't sleep, couldn't eat, that my thoughts only contained her and parts of her, that I sat in my closet and *cried* about it, that in my mind I took her apart and looked at her pieces and even now, after only a few days, I was having a hard time putting her back together as a single vision without distortions. I said, "I never liked her, man. Just trying to get some."

"That's it, dude," Mark said. "Fucking and fighting and getting fucked up." He punched the air, ducked and moved. "Fucking and fighting and getting fucked up. That's all we're about. We should start a gang. A fucking gang, dude. The fort will be our headquarters."

At the playground, twenty, maybe thirty kids stood around, all boys, ages twelve to fifteen or sixteen. Darryl stood in the middle of the open circle, punching his fist into his open hand, wearing the same ripped-up shirt he wore on the day he ate the bird. Dust blew across the playground. The swings creaked in the wind.

"Fight fight fight fight fight," all the boys shouted, some laughing and pushing each other, as Mark and I approached, Mark somehow still thinking—with the help of alcohol—that he might be able to hold his own in a fight with Darryl, who had fifty or sixty pounds on him. Even with a knife or a stick, he would have lost, would have had the knife or stick thrust right through him, as if he were no more substantial than the carcass of a bird.

This was all ridiculous, of course, the whole mess, a kind of necessary retroactive punishment. Darryl and Sissy were now boyfriend-girlfriend (for only a few weeks, it turned out). All over school property were vile slogans and epithets about Sissy. Everyone, including Sissy, knew that Mark had written them, carved them, drawn them: "Turbo-Diesel

Dyke." It wasn't that Darryl cared about Sissy—he was just hoping to have sex with her; it was that Mark had mocked and harassed something—a person, a girl, but it could have been something else, any piece of his property—that Darryl now felt was his and his alone. If anyone was going to ridicule, degrade, humiliate, or violate Sissy, it was going to be Darryl—and Darryl would do all those things soon. And Darryl was also pissed at Mark and me for leaving him under the porch at the house that day, where he woke up in darkness among insects and dust, half-covered in the sticks and pine cones we threw at him. (I was safe from him only because I had a brother tougher and bigger than he was.)

As we neared the open circle, neared Darryl with his mustached snarl, his big fists, his hair, I backed away from Mark and settled into the yelling like all the rest of the boys. Mark had to enter the fight arena, formed of young male bodies, alone. This was part of the ritual of THE FIGHT, and there were FIGHTS all the time.

Mark started screaming, screaming as loud as he could, nonsensical gibberish. His armor of amateur pornographic Polaroids taken by his father flapped in the wind, caught bits and dots of sun and threw them around in our faces.

I'm not going to describe most of what happened next, though it is, I suppose, the *dénouement*, our climax. We live in a violent culture, it goes without saying. But you don't need someone interrupting the narrative flow and getting all *soapboxy* about it. And if you have ever had a fist hit you just below the eye, on the hard bone there, or had a boot on your neck, or had a belt across your back, your ass, your legs, or had a foot striking you as you scurried away on all fours, or if you have ever had the wind knocked out of you by a knee or an elbow or a fist, or had your head dunked in a toilet until you squirmed and screamed bubbles, or had your teeth cracked in your mouth so that you feel and taste their sandy residue on your tongue, or if you have ever had the explosion of pain—literally the stars—that comes when a fist or a stick or a bottle crashes into your nose, bending cartilage, breaking bone, or if you have ever been undressed in a way you do not wish in front of a mocking audience of boys, all rabidly homophobic yet interested in shoving their cocks and balls up toward your face for a laugh, their genitals turned to weapons, or if you have ever been tied up or taped up in a basement by kids bigger than you, laughing kids, or if you have ever had the back of your skull smashed against the ground while tufts of your hair are ripped from your scalp, if you have experienced even *one* of these things, then you already know about the distance and distortion of most of the violence we see, which we can watch in our recliners. And if you have experienced even *one* of these things, then maybe you already know about the blunt banality and quick stupidity of real violence, about that room I mentioned earlier, the one where the door is locked and the devil's stereo is on and it is so tiring to either fear or hate all the time and how that kind of thing burns a little ulcer in your soul and how that kind of ulcer can be contagious, *is* contagious, gets passed on to others so that they might one day know about the room and the devil's stereo and later, some years later, not be able to help themselves from locking someone else up in that room because they've been immersed in the banality and stupidity of violence, have been *shaped* by the banality and stupidity of violence, and they have an ulcerated soul, a soul—maybe this is all I'm really trying to say—full of holes. And if you have experienced any of these things, then you also already know that what Mark wanted, all Mark really wanted at this moment, because he was a kid shaped by the blunt banality and quick stupidity of real violence, just as I was a kid partially shaped by the blunt banality and quick stupidity of real violence, was for everyone to know that he was a tough

tough tough tough tough tough tough tough tough tough
tough tough tough tough tough tough tough tough tough
tough tough tough tough tough tough tough tough tough
tough tough tough tough tough tough tough tough tough
tough tough tough tough tough tough tough tough tough
tough tough tough tough tough tough tough tough tough
tough tough tough tough tough tough tough tough tough
tough tough tough tough tough tough tough tough tough
tough tough tough tough tough tough tough tough tough
tough tough tough tough tough tough tough tough tough
tough tough tough tough tough tough tough tough tough
tough tough tough tough tough tough tough tough tough
tough tough tough tough tough tough tough tough tough
tough tough tough tough tough tough tough tough tough
tough tough tough tough tough tough tough tough tough
tough tough tough tough tough tough tough tough tough
tough *motherfucker*.

There were no surprises in the fight between Darryl and
Mark, if you could call it a fight, no interesting angles or
slow-motion shots; none of the good moves were replayed
five or six times for clarification or viewing pleasure while
someone explained them. Darryl picked Mark up over his
head, slammed him mercilessly onto the hard, gravelly dirt,
and beat his face to a bloody, swollen pulp until he was tired
of doing so, until the crowd of boys—one day, men—me

included, stopped yelling "fight fight fight" and collecting all the loose pornographic photos flying in the wind and started to worry, silently, in fidgeting fashion, about whether Darryl was going to kill, actually *kill*, Mark, who was passive on the ground, arms flung out, with a face—can't you just see it?—made for punching.

I remember us walking home after the fight, Mark's arm over my shoulder, his face barely recognizable under all the swelling, large blobs of blood exploding onto the asphalt and concrete and grass as we went.

When we got to his house, no one was home and the doors were locked. It started raining. I helped him over toward the garage and we rolled open the door with a *ratatatatatatat* and he sat down on the stained concrete. He bled a small puddle from the cuts on his face, which he kept covered by his hands, the blood flowing like tears through his fingers, over his wrists, and onto the floor and out toward the lawn mower and the gas can and hedge clippers and hoes and shovels and rakes and some orange construction cones Bill used to mark off danger. I thought he needed to go to the hospital—in my memory he lost enough blood to die twice—but he said he'd be fine until Bill got home, that he'd roll up his shirt and put it on his face to stop the bleeding, that Bill had been in lots of fights in his time, that Bill would know what to do,

Bill would help out, Bill would be home soon, any time now, soon.

I had to get going, because my dad would be getting back from work at the shipyard and my mom would be getting back from the Air Force base—I was reminded by the jet plane roaring overhead—and I needed to beat them home and change out of my bloody clothes and stuff my bloody T-shirt down to the bottom of the trash. As I walked away, I could hear Mark starting to cry, and it got louder and louder, echoing inside the belly of his garage, out through the rainy streets, and I knew it was about the pain he was feeling in his face and body, about the humiliation, about the degradation, about the anger, about losing every time, over and over and over, but I also knew, even back then, even as that dimwitted kid drifting around those neighborhoods, that it was about everything else, too, *everything*, every disastrous little thing.

Memory

Mark said:

"My mom says my dad drinks and that's why the dog is wild. She's like, 'Stop drinking and pay some attention to the dog.' And then he's like, 'I don't drink.' And then she's like, 'I can't talk to you. Why do you lie? Why do you lie? It's over and you're still lying.' I hate my parents, man. I wish my mom would die sometimes."

It was winter, spring, summer. Clouds came in and it rained. We were in the woods, at the arcade, on the playground, at the abandoned farmhouse, by the pay phones at the 7-Eleven, sticking our fingers into the quarter slots.

And because he was a boy who had become a character

in a book, he rewound as he stood before me, moved backward in time, stopped so that I might have a longer look at him, so that I might try to see who he was and what and how he *meant*, and said again:

"My mom says my dad drinks and that's why I'm wild. She's like, 'Stop drinking and pay some attention to the kid.' And then he's like, 'I don't drink,' and then she's like, 'I can't talk to you. Why do you lie? Why do you lie? It's over and you're still lying.' I hate my life, man. I wish I would I could if maybe I was, you know."

Family

A few days after the fight, a little girl, maybe two years old, with curly blonde hair, was walking around inside Mark's house. She had on a heavy diaper and was carrying a yellow sippy cup. Her back was covered in dark-red mosquito bites.

"Hey, Mark," I said loudly, letting the screen door shut behind me. The kid looked at me. I looked at her. She climbed up and sat in the old blue recliner with the torn armrest and then climbed down again, as if she couldn't make up her mind about whether to sit or keep walking around the house. I noticed all the Pepsi and beer cans and liquor bottles had been picked up. In fact, the house, not exactly clean, was much neater.

Mark came out of the dark hallway, gently rubbing his blackened, swollen eyes. He had a maroon, almost black cut across the bridge of his nose. A large bandage on his forehead. "Oh, yeah," he said, seeing the kid. "That's Alex."

The little girl walked through the kitchen, into the back den.

"Who's Alex?" I said.

"Debra's kid."

"Who's Debra?"

"The woman who locked her keys in the car." He looked down the hall. Quietly: "Remember her? With the nice tits."

"Is she here?"

"She's in the back bedroom with Bill. They're sleeping."

"Who's watching the kid?"

"Her mom, I guess. I don't know."

"But she's sleeping."

"I don't know, dude. What do you want me to fucking say?"

"Someone should be watching her. She could just walk out into the street. The latch on your screen door doesn't even work."

"You can. Go in there and watch her. Sing her a happy song, idiot."

"I'm not watching her. I'm just saying."

"I guess," he said, "we can turn on some cartoons."

We walked into the den and there was the little girl sitting on the floor, flipping through a car magazine. There was no pot out, no porn laying around. Someone had vacuumed. The kid seemed happy enough. What did she know about anything? We turned on some cartoons.

Then Mark and I got three bowls of sugary cereal, one for each of us. There wasn't any milk, and all the spoons were dirty in the sink, soaking in sudsy dishwater (what genius had thought of this?), and I wasn't going to wash them and Mark wasn't going to wash them and the kid was too small to make her do it, so we just used our hands when we got back to the den. Alex sat between me and Mark on the floor, our backs against the green couch, and we watched the end of a cartoon.

After that we watched MTV—Joan Jett, the Cars, the Vapors, the Police. Alex didn't say anything. She seemed to like the colors of the music videos. She liked the cereal. A few minutes later she stood up, picked up her sippy cup, and got up close to Mark's face and started poking at his bruises, which I imagine she might have thought looked nice and colorful. She put her finger on the cut above his nose.

"Ow," he said. "No. Don't do that." The kid laughed and tried to do it again. It was a game: Make purple face say "ow." He grabbed her arms gently and turned her around so that she was sitting in his lap. She reached up over her head and touched his hair and settled into holding onto his earlobe. "Ow," he said. "Man, even my hair hurts." But he let the kid keep holding his ear while she sat on his lap watching TV.

"What did Bill say about your face?" I asked.

"He said I needed to learn how to fight. He said he'd get Rusty to teach me some more dirty fighting skills. He told me never to walk straight into a fight when the guy is ready. I think that's what happened. Darryl got that one good move at the beginning."

"Yeah," I said. "The body slam."

"I wouldn't say it was a body slam. He just picked me up."

"It was a body slam."

"Well, if he wouldn't have got that one good move, I think I would have had a chance."

"Yeah," I said. "That was a good move, that body slam. Without that, you might have gotten him. Maybe. You could have."

MTV went to a commercial. "This kid," Mark said, looking down at the top of the little girl's head, "walked around all night, man. She doesn't sleep."

We heard the bedroom door open down at the end of the hall. We heard Debra say, "Hey, sweetie, hey Alex hon, come on back here with me and Mr. Bill. Come on, hon. Come see Mr. Bill."

Alex got up with her sippy cup and waddle-ran to see her mom. She said, "Ma ma ma." She was a cute kid. I thought of my younger brother, who was seven and in day care across town. He had blond hair like that. When he was Alex's age, he used to get on my chest and put his hands in my mouth and look down my throat. He wanted to know what was inside a person, what was inside me. It was a great mystery, the essence of people, like staring down into a hole. He used to say, "It's dark in you. I can't see! I can't see!" I felt some quick surge like memory, like love, like an unbearable ache for a place to call home, in my throat, up behind my eyes. For a split second I couldn't see, couldn't swallow. Everything went black.

Then I came back. Mark was still staring at the TV. He said, "I think my dad might marry Debra."

"Really?" I said. "I didn't think he liked her. I thought he just fucked her."

"Yeah," he said. "But my mom's a dyke. She'll freak when she hears Bill has a new wife and a little girl, a stepkid. I'm not going to talk to my mom anymore. I'm getting out of here as soon as I can work a job. I got an uncle down in Florida, man. One day I might write my mom a letter about how great it is to be a big brother, or to live with my uncle in Florida and make my own money. I think I will. I can just see her face when she reads it. It's going to kill her."

"Where's Debra's car, that blue Mustang?" I asked. "It wasn't in the driveway."

"I don't know," Mark said, staring again at the TV, a new video coming on.

"That was a cool car," I said.

"Yeah," he said. "Her car is pretty awesome. That's something. Maybe she'll let me drive it if she ends up being my new mom."

We watched more TV. When the next commercial came on, I said, "Want to do something?"

"Nah," he said.

"Why not?" I said.

He waited a few seconds. He started to say something, a lie, I would guess, but stopped himself. Then he looked right at me, two clear eyes set deep in all that injury, and said, "Because I don't want anyone to see my face."